The Best of Shrdlu

ABCDEFGHIJKLMNOPQRSTUVWXYZ

Denys Parsons

The Best of Shrdlu

Pan Original
Pan Books London and Sydney

First published 1981 by Pan Books Ltd,
Cavaye Place, London SW10 9PG
© Denys Parsons 1981
ISBN 0 330 26375 7
Printed and bound in Great Britain by
Cox and Wyman Ltd, Reading

Introduction

Gobfrey Shrdlu is the malicious spirit with an irrepressible sense of humour who lurks at the elbow of tired journalists and printers with disastrous consequences. 'FATHER OF TEN SHOT DEAD – MISTAKEN FOR RABBIT' typifies for me Shrdlu's genius and for the last thirty years I have been keeping track of his exploits and bringing them to public notice. It is of course Shrdlu who mixes letters ('While your partner is dealing you should be snuffling'), who adds unwanted commas ('This appliance will reduce your hips, or bust'), and who puts words in an unfortunate order ('Lost – small red-faced lady's wristwatch'), and there is some evidence, too, that Shrdlu is responsible for the bizarre incidents which strain credulity beyond the limit, and exemplified by 'Man bites horse' or 'Man lost leg as he opened cash register'. Anyhow, I have as usual displayed for your enjoyment misprints and the like (Funny Ha Ha) on left-hand pages, and the odd news stories (Funny Peculiar) on right-hand pages.

I am sometimes asked whether I invent any of the items, and the answer is an emphatic 'No'. Surely many of the best are self-evidently genuine: 'Lonely lady, 43, with little dog, seeks post', and 'Magistrates may act on indecent shows'. Who could have sat down to make these up deliberately?

'Do you spend all day reading newspapers?' is another question I am often asked. No, I found some of the items myself, but many I took at second-hand from journals such as *Punch* and *New Yorker* who used such items as fill-ins at the bottom of pages. Others have been sent to me by keen shrdlologists, in particular by Patrick Moore, the astronomer, Mary Pearce of Iver, and Edward North of Sidcup.

The Best of Shrdlu is an omnibus edition comprising one quarter of new material and three-quarters of favourite items culled from my previous Shrdlu books. The full list of these, for the information of Shrdlu fans all over the world, is as follows: *It Must Be True* (1952), *Can it be True?* (1953), *All Too True* (1954), *True to Type* (1955), *Many a True Word* (1958), *Never More True* (1960), (all published by Macdonald & Co in hardback). *Funny Ha Ha & Funny Peculiar* (1965), *Funny Ho Ho & Funny Fantastic* (1967), *Funny Amusing & Funny Amazing* (1969), *Funny Convulsing and Funny Confusing* (1971), *Funny Funny Funny* (1976), *Funny Ribtickleous & Funny Ridiculous* (1979) (all Pan original paperbacks); *Fun-tastic* (1971), *Even More Fun-tastic* (1972), (both Pan Piccolo). *Nothing Brightens the Garden like Primrose Pants* (1955, Hanover House, New York), and *Say it isn't so* (1962, A. S. Barnes & Co, New York). All these books are out of print except some of the Funny Ha Ha series which Pan keep reprinting in response to demand.

Ho there! *The Best of Shrdlu* is indeed the best – from a lifetime of following the misdeeds of Gobfrey Shrdlu. As Shrdlu would say, 'This is a treat you must not fail to miss.' Read on and laugh your head off.

The Best of Shrdlu

Some members of the Kindler Foundation seemed somewhat open-mouthed and stunned by the novelty of the work, but they were also rather tight-lipped.

Washington Post

We see sexual promiscuity as a prime factor in increasing our divorce rate and in undermining mahogany which we believe to be basic to our social structure.

Richmond News Leader (Virginia)

Q. How can I repair cigarette burns in furniture upholstery?
A. Select a yarn to match the colour of the damaged upholstery, and darn the hole with close stitches. Then place it in a heavy paper bag and keep it in a moderately cold section of your refrigerator.

Highland Park News-Herald (California)

Asked whether he had any regrets over his action, speaking softly in broken English, he replied 'No'.

Sunday Post (Glasgow)

GROUNDBREAKING. Construction begins at the New Canaan's luxury townhouse project, Canaan Close, with the excavation of Miss Jane Matthews, Fairfield County columnist.

Westport News (Connecticut)

After removing the meat from your broiling pan allow it to soak in soapy water.

Seattle Post-Intelligence

A man was treated for burns and bruising after clinging to the luggage rack on the boot of a car for 10 kilometres as it sped through Brisbane streets. His ordeal ended when the sports car crashed into the rear of a taxi which had been pursuing it. The man told police that he leapt on to the boot of the car when it was taken from his home in Ashgrove. He had not been able to get off because his foot was stuck. Police took no action when they learned the driver was the man's wife.

Melbourne Age

Marie who lives in Audley Range said today: 'I have wanted to be a gnome ever since I read in a magazine article about what people's reactions might be to a real live gnome.'

Lancashire Evening Telegraph

My bridegroom's first words to me at the altar when I joined him were: 'Who are you?' It made me think that the hours I spent on myself before going to church were all worth while.

Letter in *Daily Mirror*

An ad they will discontinue is the one on a black background saying: 'I thought the Kama Sutra was an Indian restaurant until I discovered Smirnoff.' Mr Ambler explained: 'We made a survey and found 60 per cent of people did think it was an Indian restaurant.'

Evening News

Aunts in the house are a serious nuisance and are not easily expelled once they have established a kingdom. Perhaps a chemist in your town could help you.

People's Friend

If you shoot yourself and have not used Blank's ammunition, you have missed one of the pleasures of life.

Advert in Birmingham paper

A familiar question was re-opened – How Sunday School children are to be attached to the Church, and once more the use of adhesive stamps was recommended.

New Zealand Church News

A big music store in the centre of Louisville has been completely burned out. The brigade played on the burning instruments for many hours.

Northern Daily Mail

Prisoners in London who go to court with groundless appeals will risk serving extra time. Lord Parker, the Chief Justice, gave this warning recently when he announced a new plan to discourage frivolous cases which are jamming the legal machine.

Slowly lean forward and put the top of your head into the saucer.

Straighten your legs and walk them towards your body.

Baltimore Sun

Sex education in primary school has always been a controversial subject, especially when accompanied by demonstration. Last week Fan Man-mei gave birth to a baby girl while teaching her third grade class at Kunghuan Primary School. No further demonstrations are planned for the immediate future.

Teipei Economic News

Post Office workers at Folkestone sorting office called police on Monday when they discovered a vibrating parcel. The police found that the parcel contained vibrating breast developers, one of which had been activated.

Folkestone and Hythe Gazette

Mrs Daisy Enford, mother of three children and married for 17 years called to her husband in the garden, 'I am getting a divorce,' it was stated in the Family Division of the High Court yesterday. The husband replied: 'If I do not get these tomato plants in soon they will die.'

The Times

'I was with Ian while he was at the Club. He is not uncontrollable. He is big, but then boys are bigger than girls. None of the other mothers complained to me. Ian did shut Mrs Carter's little girl in a trunk. He's a naturally tidy child and puts all things away.'

Birmingham Post

After viewing the headless, armless, and legless torso, Coroner Marvin Rogers and Coast Guard Captain Willie E. Carr both voiced the opinion that the 65-year-old real estate agent had been slain.

Philadelphia Inquirer

Two previous studies using the same analytical model have shown that the unconstrained optimum calls for the aircraft to dive underground during both the initial acceleration after take-off and the final deceleration down to landing. In *this* work the aircraft has been constrained not to descend below the ground.

Journal of the Aircraft

> Opal-diamond ring, set in
> Hoovermatic de luxe twin
> tub, £650 ono
>
> *Evening Echo* (Bournemouth)

Thieves stole 600 loaves of bread from an empty delivery van yesterday.   *Sun*

Grandad, 2 litre GL, 1976, 35,000 miles, spotless condition, price £3,800.

Evening Press (Dublin)

Earlier in the evening, Marita had another exciting moment in a raffle – her mother was picked out of a hat.

Irish Press

If you take your dog in the car don't let him hang out of a window while driving.

Daily Mirror

The Gentle Art of Housebreaking by Australian horse-woman Robbie Murray is a helpful and easily read book giving a real insight into many of the problems that arise.

Evening News (Hereford)

COMPONENT CORPORATIONS OF COMPONENT
CORPORATIONS – If a corporation is a component corporation of an acquiring corporation, under subsection (b)
or under this subsection, it shall (except for the purposes of
section 742d and section 743a) also be a component corporation of the corporation of which such acquiring corporation is a component corporation.

American Revenue Act of 1940

He told the bench last week: 'I went to Sutton police
station to tell police a stranger had called inquiring about
my brother's address. I was wary because my brother was
away and I wanted the police to call at my brother's house
to check. But the police seemed unwilling to check that the
stranger was not someone about to annoy my brother's
wife. I think the fact that I manufacture door knobs may
have something to do with it.'

Sutton and Cheam Herald

A post-mortem on a parakeet from a council house in
Kingsbridge showed that it had died from psittacosis. The
bird was bought from a pet shop in the Plymouth area two
weeks before it died. Enquiries into its origin have not been
finalized because the supplier of the bird is unavailable for
comment. He has been bitten by a poisonous snake.

South Devon Journal

An American musician, Eddie Purvis, who was found in a
doorway holding a hammer, screwdriver and spanner at
3.50 a.m. on Tuesday told police: 'I was just going to make
a guitar.'

Croydon Advertiser

Mr Brown spoke of a possible giant from the Department of the Environment for repairing the clock.

Western Gazette (Yeovil)

He gets every anonymous letter that is sent in and sees to it that the writers are answered.

New York Times

Morning dress or uniform will be worn at the ceremony. Mayors are requested to wear their chains of office only.

Instructions issued by Manchester Corporation

KING WILLIAM'S TOWN – Riotous conduct. Lizzie Mengwe pleaded guilty to creating a disturbance in Bridge Street by eating her mother, and was sentenced to fourteen days' hard labour.

Cape Mercury

The outstanding characteristic of the dog is its honesty. In love or hate, joy or sorrow, a dog is sincere. It will not bite your hand or wag its tail unless it likes you.

Sporting Weekly

At the end of the service the choir will sing a special anthem composed by the organist, after which the church will be closed for necessary repairs.

Canadian paper

To relieve the monotony of sitting, the audience are asked to rise during the rendering of the Chorus: 'Fix'd in His everlasting seat'.

Choir Festival programme

MRS VICKERY GETS A STEAM-ROLLER
FOR HER BIRTHDAY

HOUSEWIFE Mrs Betty Vickery went for a driving lesson
yesterday – on a six-ton steam-roller. Mother-of-four Mrs
Vickery was given the 1907 Aveling and Porter road roller
as a surprise birthday present by her husband, garage
owner Mr Alan Vickery.

Now she's practising 'like mad' for her test so that she can
drive it to traction engine rallies. Steam-rollers run in the
family. Her father, Mr Frank Pratley, 73, earned his living
for almost 50 years driving them. He took her for her lesson
yesterday – a 5 mph trip down the High Street at Harpen-
den, Hertfordshire.

At home in Snatchup, Redbourn, Hertfordshire, Mrs
Vickery, 32, said: 'It takes an hour to work up steam and
1 cwt of coal lasts only five miles.' Mr Vickery said: 'I
spotted the steam-roller at a garage at High Wycombe, in
Buckinghamshire, and I realized it would be just the thing
for my wife.'   *Daily Mail*

**There were murmurs of disapproval from a defence
solicitor. Mr Peter Smith, prosecuting for Havering
Council, rose to inform puzzled magistrates: 'I
think my friend is disturbed because the witness
has taken the oath on a steak and kidney pie.'**
                                          Hornchurch Echo

A *Phocaena phocaena* was found today propped up in one of
the cubicles of the men's lavatory in Glasgow Central
station. The staff thought it was a dolphin, but the 4 ft 64 lb
carcass was identified as a porpoise by the museums' department at Kelvingrove Park. How it had come into the
lavatory nobody knew: one gentleman said: 'We had heavy
rain and there was flooding, but this is ridiculous.'
                                             The Times

Iron oxide is used to make those very dark-coloured bottles in which those of us who can remember champagne used to be packed.

Wine Trade paper

After you have switched off you are now ready to connect up the four wires. But don't try to connect the wife between A and B or you may get a shock.

Electrical paper

RICHARD BURTON, who plays the lead, and Elizabeth Taylor (who doesn't) arrived in Mexico City to be greeted by 1,500 screaming fans. With them were Lisa Todd, Miss Taylor's daughter by the late Mike Todd and several assistants.

Daily Mail

GIRLS READY TO WEAR CLOTHING
Notice in General Store

Those who have not heard the Duchess speak are always captivated by the beauty of her voice.

Scots paper

GARDENING AND LIVESTOCK. Will all clients of Miss S— please note that she is leaving town. No further stripping.

Newcastle Journal

Sidmouth warden, Mr Henry Y— needed help to maintain order and indecency in public places.

Pulman's Weekly News

*Federal Rules Decision, Grau v. Procter & Gamble Co.,
United States District Court, M.D. Alabama N.D.*

On January 8 1963, the official court reporter for this district filed with the Clerk of this Court a certified transcript of the proceedings in this case. Subsequent to the filing of the original certified transcript by the court reporter, the defendants, now the appellees, asked this Court to strike and eliminate certain portions thereof. The exact portions of the record which this Court is asked to strike are as follows:

Page 24: 'Mr Garrett: Ha, ha, ha, ha.'

* * * * * * * * * *

'Mr Garrett: Ha, ha, ha, ha.'

Page 42: 'Q (Mr Garrett): Ha, ha, ha, ha.'

* * * * * * * * * *

'Q (Mr Garrett): Ha, ha, ha.'

Page 74: 'Q (Mr Garrett): Ha, ha.'

Page 82: 'Mr Garrett: Ha, ha, ha.'

Page 105: 'Mr Garrett: Ha, ha, ha, ha.'

'Juror: Ha, ha, ha.'

In asking this Court to edit the record and strike the above portions, the appellees state 'that although Mr Garrett and the juror may have made some sound at such times, that it was an inadvertent mannerism, such as a person coughing, clearing his throat or otherwise inadvertently making a sound'. The appellees contend that the inclusion of the above portions of the proceeding merely serve to clutter unduly the record on appeal in this case. The plaintiff, now the appellant, formally objects to altering or changing the official transcript.

New Yorker

Constable John Knight told the Court that on 30 June David Durbin had said to him: 'I'll kill you.' 'Did he kill you?' asked the prosecutor, Mr H. A. Kelly.

Rand Daily Mail

Gaudy cottons for garden and country are striped like a zebra in scarlet, blue, green, yellow, and purple.

Daily Sketch

'Today', she said, and he held up his thumb and grinned at her. If only this could be for ever, the two of them alone. But the sea lifted the boat like a sullen cork, and he stopped thinking about anything but handling her.

John Bull

MATINS

Hymn 43 'Great God, what do I see and hear?'
Preacher Rev. Dr Bernard Taylor.
Hymn 45 'Hark! an awful voice is sounding.'

Church notice-board

Ghana is to change over to driving on the right. The change will be made gradually.

Ghana Paper

INSTRUCTIONS
Pour a teaspoonful of the
shampoo into the palm
of each hand ...

Label on bottle

No authenticated case has been known in which sterile parents have transmitted that quality to their offspring.

Letter to *The Times*

SANTA ANA, CALIFORNIA – Johnny Whiteside, an unemployed clown, was arrested Saturday after police found him sharing his 35-foot trailer home with three 160–200 pound bears, a burro, a wallaby, an ocelot, a bobcat, three goats, two opossums, a monkey, three peacocks and his wife.

Bangor News (Maine)

A High Street dentist wanted his property down-valued because customers of the Chinese 'take-away' next door spilt sweet-and-sour sauce on the footpath. As the sauce looked like blood it was putting people off coming to his practice.

Estates Times

The case was adjourned because the victim of the assault required a steel plate to be inserted in his head. The defending solicitor told the court that his client should be ready for the case to resume in a month 'if he is not affected by the steel strike'.

Western Mail

Mrs Maria Thompson was so incensed after her husband had bitten her on the buttocks that she tried to jump on him from a first floor window as he left the house.

Hartlepool Mail

Gillian dialled 999 from a telephone in her home, but unfortunately she shouted 'Fire' to the GPO operator and hung up. Mr Geoffrey Maples, forty-three, said: 'We are proud of the way Gillian acted. It was only a fortnight ago that she was allowed to start playing games.'

Daily Telegraph

It's all very well for the promoters of new hair fashions who use girls with gorgeous tresses for their ideas, but who cares about birds with lank, thin hair, or those with stiff, straight bristols.

Western Evening Herald

Many diabetic children learn quickly how to give themselves injections. Almost all are skilled in the procedure by the time they are tight.

The Times

After consuming about a hundred portions of chips, 28 pounds of sausages, rolls, ice cream and cake, Mrs Morgan presented the trophies won by the boys.

Local paper

The harbour and Long Island Sound were covered thick with ice and a large number of transatlantic steamers could not get in. Traffic was almost at a standstill. In a village near New York a woman was found in bed beside her husband.

Neue Würzburger Zeitung

The font so generously presented by Mrs Smith will be set in position at the East end of the Church. Babies may now be baptised at both ends.

Surrey paper

Owing to a plague of wasps in the Sheffield district, farmers have had to stop harvest operations to take wasps wasp nests before they could gather in their wasps.

Edinburgh Evening Dispatch

A shepherd's wife, Mrs Jean Driver, of North Farm near Berwick, could not understand why a piece of coal at the front of her blazing coal fire was not burning. She took it out to find that it was an eight-inch stick of gelignite. Mrs Driver, who has three children, said, 'We could have been blown to bits. I will certainly mention it to the coalman when he makes his next delivery.'

Scotsman

RABBIT IN MIXER SURVIVES

A baby rabbit fell into a quarry's mixing machine yesterday and came out in the middle of a concrete block. But the rabbit still had the strength to dig its way free before the block set.

The tiny creature was scooped up with 30 tons of sand, then swirled and pounded through the complete mixing process. Mr Michael Hooper, the machine operator, found the rabbit shivering on top of the solid concrete block, its coat stiff with fragments. A hole from the middle of the block and paw marks showed the escape route.

Mr Reginald Denslow, manager of J. R. Pratt and Sons' quarry at Kilmington, near Axminster, Devon, said: 'This rabbit must have a lot more than nine lives to go through this machine. I just don't know how it avoided being suffocated, ground, squashed or cut in half.' With the 30 tons of sand, it was dropped into a weighing hopper and carried by conveyor to an overhead mixer where it was whirled around with gallons of water.

From there the rabbit was swept to a machine which hammers wet concrete into blocks by pressure of 100 lb per square inch. The rabbit was encased in a block 18 inches long, nine inches high and six inches thick. Finally the blocks were ejected on to the floor to dry and the dazed rabbit clawed itself free. 'We cleaned him up, dried him by the electric fire, then he hopped away,' Mr Denslow said.

Daily Telegraph

At about one o'clock when the eclipse was on the sun, I saw a most beautiful star shining very bright, and I pointed this out to three ladies who were watching the eclipse in a bath of water. Is this an unusual occurrence?

Letter in West London paper

'Mr Perkins might be able to help you,' she said, as she took down a dusty lodger from a shelf.

Weekly magazine serial

Miss Goldhurst has NO MALE GOAT this season, and refers all clients to Mr Harris.

Advert in *Grantham Journal*

MARSEILLES. Seaman Marcel Rivien has won a breach-of-promise suit brought against him by redhead Noelle Michel. He told the court he could not marry a girl with 12 tattoos on her chest.

Weekend

'PREGNANT' FOR 37 YEARS
By Our Rome Correspondent

A peasant woman aged 72 carried an unborn eight months old baby in her body for 37 years without being aware of it, Prof. Vito de Palma, chief obstetrician of the Termoli Hospital, Campobasso, in South Italy, disclosed yesterday.

He said that the woman, named only as Maria T. came to his surgery a few days ago complaining of stomach pains. X-rays revealed the presence of an eight months old child whose body was completely fossilized.

Daily Telegraph

LAST MONDAY a garage fitted a new radio aerial to my car. I have now discovered that I have five different ways of turning off my radio. They are: (1) by operating the foot brake; (2) by changing gear; (3) by touching the loudspeaker cover; (4) by tapping the speedometer glass; and (5) the on-off switch.

I also find that I can increase the volume by operating the heater control. I doubt if any of the expensive cars at this year's Motor Show have such an elaborate radio system incorporated!

Letter in *Sunday Mirror*

My hubby sells Christmas cards in his shop. Every year he picks one from the shelf, gives it to me – without writing on it – and then asks me to put it back when I've read it.

Letter in *Daily Mirror*, quoted in *New Statesman*

Lie flat on the back, with the feet tucked under the wardrobe. Keep the hands at the sides and raise the legs until they are vertical. Very slowly lower again.

South African paper

Asked if they supported women's lib, 47.5% said they did, 44.3% said they did not, and 8.2% had no opinion. Broken down by sex, 48.9% of the men favoured the movement, compared to only 45.4% of the women.

New York News

LUCIO SILVEIRA, 30, fell asleep on a heap of pitch left by road workers in Sao Paulo and woke up as a statue. The warmth of his body softened the pitch and he sank deeper and deeper until only his head and shoulders were showing. When he awoke the pitch had solidified and he looked like a bust mounted on a black base.

The fire brigade cut a block out of the pitch and carted Lucio to hospital, where nurses took more than an hour to remove the pitch.

Guardian

AIDING AND ABETTING

In Thornton *v*. Mitchell the driver of an omnibus had to reverse it. In order to do so, he relied upon the signals of the conductor. The conductor gave the driver the signal to reverse, which he did, and two pedestrians were knocked down. The driver was summoned for driving without due care and attention and the conductor for aiding and abetting. The case against the driver was dismissed and it was held that the conductor could not be found guilty of aiding and abetting in the commission of an offence which had not been committed.

Introduction to Criminal Law by Cross & Jones

SUICIDE BULLET KILLS BABY

HITZKIRCH, Switzerland, Wednesday – A 57-year-old man shot himself near here today, the bullet passing through his head, through the ceiling and killing his baby grand-daughter sleeping on the floor above.

Evening Standard

'Ever green' was Sir Joseph Sykes Rymer's jocular reference to the new Lord Mayor and Lady Mayoress in his speech proposing the election of the Lord Mayor, and not 'very green', as given in our issue of yesterday.

Yorkshire Herald

OTTAWA – The Canadian Government invited five US oil company executives to Ottawa, Wednesday, gave them lunch and discussed prospects for a cross-Canada pipeline for crêpes suzettes.

Dallas Times Herald

Observing the temporary incapacity of Mr Lea who seemed to be thinking furiously with his mouth open, Mr Swift MacNeill filled the aching void.

Liverpool Courier

It is reported from Bedfordshire that the Foreign Secretary, who is undergoing treatment, has had a less restful night. Swine fever has broken out.

Evening Standard

> *Mr Jones is wrong to suggest that I support the rich against the poor. To the Christian there is no class distinction – that idea was largely concocted by the working classes.*

Letter in *Reynolds News*

This place is the preferred resort for those wanting solitude. People searching for such solitude are in fact flocking here from all corners of the globe.

Swiss resort prospectus

'The Albert Hall Orchestra', it seems, means one thing to the proprietors of the building opposite the Albert Memorial in Kensington, and another thing to Mr Albert Edward Hall, who founded, owned and named an orchestra of this description. The proprietors of the Hall sought an injunction to restrain Mr Hall from using the name so as to induce the public to believe that his orchestra was so connected with the building. But they failed; for the orchestra was small, Mr Hall honest, the proprietors of the Hall had no orchestra themselves, and there was no evidence of injury to them. Mr Hall evidently owed much to parental foresight at the font.

Miscellany-at-Law by R. E. Megarry

STEAM-ROLLER IN DISTRESS
STARTS A SCARE AT SEA

As the storm which ravaged the south blew itself out last night a full-scale air-sea rescue operation was ordered in the Bristol Channel for the survivors of an air crash. All shipping was warned to look out. Coatguards watched. Lifeboat crews stood by. A Shackleton crew at RAF St Mawgan, Cornwall, prepared to take off as soon as the weather cleared.

But the alarm was called off – when police traced the distress call to a road roller on the M5 between Almondsbury and Cribbs Causeway, six miles north of Bristol. The driver, unable to work in the storm, had signalled to his mates two miles up the road:

'Mayday. Weather terrible. Am ditching for tonight.'

The international distress signal was picked up by radio ham Mr Ray Smith of Patchway, Bristol. He rang the police, the police rang the airports. ... A spokesman for Gloucestershire police said last night: 'The driver who sent the message is an ex-RAF radio operator.'

Daily Mail

FLORIDA GIRL LOSES 79 lbs

'I was the hippiest girl in weight naturally. Without town,'
said Wanda Dawson of harmful drugs, too Ayds are
Jacksonville, Florida, when she available in a chewy vanilla
weighed 223 lbs. Her husband caramel, in a plain chocolate
even called her a short bale of fudge type and a minty
choco-cotton. Finally her boss lady late fudge.

Advert in Binghampton Evening Press

He had been aware from the first that she was unusually
attractive; now, in her dark green dress with the low-cut,
rounded neckline, he saw that she had lovely legs.

From The Jade Venus by G. H. Coxe

In the last two rounds both threw non-stop punches to the
acclaim of an enthusiastic audience, but the British boy was
hitting the cleaner.

Evening Standard

**E. Cramer Ltd require beamer, presser and girl for
stripping.**

Long Eaton Advertiser

Almost from the start the race developed into a two-man
battle, and over the last three miles they ran shoulder to
shoulder, with the Yorkshire man always that yard in front.

Sunday paper

The manufacturers of this sock MUST be washed in LUKE-
WARM water, NOT HOT, and well rinsed to remove soap.

Instructions with Pearlustra socks

WHY I HAD NAIL IN MY HEAD
by SEAMAN

SEAMAN Michael Fish, 36, told detectives yesterday that he asked friends to drive a two-inch nail into his head to stop a headache.

He said he had been drinking with them in a Southampton public house and felt a bout of migraine coming on.

Mr Fish added: 'It felt as if I had a bubble in my head ready to burst and so I asked the chaps with me to bang a nail through my skull. They agreed.'

The men went outside, found a nail and hammered it into his head with a piece of wood.

'After that the headache completely disappeared and I felt better altogether.'

Mrs Patsy Marsh, of Alma Terrace, Southampton, who met Mr Fish in a public house, said last night: 'He was a stranger to me. He told me he had found a cure for headaches and showed me the top of a nail sticking out of his skull. He said it had happened two hours before at a party.'

Mrs Marsh went to hospital with him. He was then taken to the Atkinson Morley's Hospital, Wimbledon, London, where the nail was removed. Back at the Royal South Hampshire Hospital in Southampton he told his story yesterday.

A police spokesman said: 'There is no question of black magic being involved in any way. We are still continuing our investigations. But the man is completely happy about the whole affair, says that he does not know the name of the person who banged the nail in his head, and wants no action taken.'   *Daily Mail*

A motor horse-box carrying a live horse can travel at 30 mph. If the horse dies in transit the vehicle immediately becomes a carrier of horseflesh and by law must reduce speed to 20 mph.   *Daily Mail*

A pot-luck dinner was held at the city park, one block north of the museum, as a fund-raising event to finance further repairs and improvements to Mrs Charles Seeger, museum committee Chairman.

Portland Oregonian

Order chicken cut into serving pieces. Clean as necessary. Wash, drain, and blot on absorbent paper. Place chicken in deep bowl. Mash in a mortar the garlic, oregano, salt and peppercorns. Add to rum, mixed with soy sauce. Pour over children.

Ridgewood (New Jersey) Record

Dear Madam,
    I am sorry that your gas installation does not give you an adequate supply of hot water. I will go into this with you as soon as convenient.

Letter from Wilts gas company

The Cape Hatteras region, developed as America's first national seashore park, was visited by 306,328 persons, three times the attendance for the previous year when no attendance figures were kept.

American magazine

At Petty Sessions, Francis Beestrup was fined 25s for allowing his dog to be unmuzzled and for being at large without a collar.

Essex paper

The plaintiff, giving evidence, said that when he was on the crossing in Chertsey Street, Guildford, he heard a shout. He turned and saw the cow coming pell-mell round a corner. It trampled over him and continued on its way. He did not think it deliberately went for him.

MR PATRICK O'CONNOR, for King Bros., submitted that the person in control of a tame animal *mansuetae naturae* – and a cow was undoubtedly tame – was not liable for damage done by it which was 'foreign to its species'. He would seek to prove the cow attacked the plaintiff; if that were so, there was no liability.

HIS LORDSHIP – Is one to abandon every vestige of common sense in approaching this matter?

COUNSEL – Yes, my Lord.

The hearing was adjourned.

The Times

YOUNG BUSINESS GIRL would like another girl to share her furnished apartment. Must squeeze toothpaste from the bottom. Write Miss F. G. Box 440, Benington, Vermont.

Benington Evening Banner

A Liberal undertaker writes: 'I cannot get Tories to give me any money for the Liberal Party whilst they are alive, so I am adding £1 to their funeral expenses.'

Liberal News

Gray pleaded guilty to stealing one hundredweight of liquid milk chocolate. He said he wanted to be reconciled to his wife who got a separation order yesterday, so he thought he would get her some chocolate.

Evening Standard

Plaintiff further said that he was afraid they might try and poison him; such things had been done before.

After a consultation this was effected, and the Stipendiary said he was pleased to hear it.

Pontypridd Observer

By that simple and dishonest device, he forced the British to reopen talks they had concluded. Sir Alec, like Harold Wilson after him, was to scratch his head at the anticssbfszyus strange man who dusbfe thing andszbwd the world Prtss he wassdoing the the oppposite.

Australasian

Time and again the Scots found space down the left. Hughes was not a great deal more reassuring, his lack of a left foot again being apparent.

Sunday Times

The coffee house will have the services of two efficient 'captains' and twelve polite and courteous waitresses, specially selected for their experiences, to attend to customers.

Straits Times

FOR SALE. Three-piece suite.
Settee turns into bed covered in thick
yellow mustard.

Midlands paper

This rule was included as a concession solely to cover the position of members who died whilst they were away on sick leave at reduced rates. It was contemplated that they would pay up any arrears on return to duty.

Civil Service Opinion

'I don't know whether or not I am the father of the child. I am only an apprentice,' wrote a man to the Woking Bench in answer to a summons against him for an affiliation order.

Woking Herald

What nonsense to suggest, as your women's page did last week, that the use of a dummy is either unhygienic or a bad habit which could become hard for baby to break. I have derived great comfort from my dummy for over 40 years, and find it gives much greater oral satisfaction than the unhealthy cigarette. It is also much cheaper.

Letter in *Brighton & Hove Herald*

Dandruff may be contracted by resting the head against infected upholstery in railway carriages, I suggest, therefore, that railway carriages should be boiled for twenty minutes at each station or halt.

Letter in *Daily Mirror*

Two men got a long ladder and placed it against the window. A woman of 14 stone was the first to start the descent. And she set off down the ladder head first. She was prevailed upon to return and go down in the normal way.

Report in *Daily Mirror*

PROBATION

At Frome yesterday Mrs Jennifer Ann Green of Kean Street,
Frome, was placed on probation for three years for stealing
the Gas Board.

Bath Evening Chronicle

LIVESTOCK FOR SALE – Pedigree Mare, in perfect
condition, hard body, fold away base. What offers?

Drogheda Independent

Amid the cheers of their many friends in the farming community the bride and groom cut the wedding cake made by
Mrs Luston (shaped like a haystack on stilts).

Dayton, Ohio, paper quoted in *Evening Standard*

Any experienced bridge player will realize that the message
South has conveyed is this: 'I see probable game. It may be
in Spades or in Hearts, or it may be in No Trumps, or perhaps in a minor suit.'

Sunday paper

AUSTIN 1100 1967, 24,000 miles,
service certificate, lady under radio,
extras, £485.

Advert in *Southern Evening Echo*

Recent animals at the Grand Hotel include Mr and Mrs
Hayes.

Buenos Aires Herald

The fact that West Wickham fire station is situated in a road which is blocked at both ends was mentioned by the Secretary of Hayes Village Association on Thursday last week.

Kentish Times

All my life I have suffered from very hairy ears. Two years ago a friend told me that this was because I was a Liberal. This so impressed me that I joined the Socialist Party, and now I have very hairy backs to my hands too.

Letter in the *Daily Mail*

'People,' he commented, 'don't hang from their bedroom windows late at night, screaming for some considerable time, because they cannot have relations with their wives.' He thought it had been proved that this was what Mr W— had done.

News of the World

A SKITTISH Northern lady who would prefer to be nameless arrived home the other day to find her husband working on his car. He was lying underneath it with his legs sticking out and as she passed she said 'Hello, darling,' and gave him what you might call an intimate squeeze.

She then proceeded in high spirits into the house, where, to her horror and astonishment, she met her husband in the hall. Meanwhile the man next door had sustained a wound to his forehead that required three stitches. He found it hard to explain to HIS wife why he had banged his head so hard on the underside of his neighbour's car.

Evening Standard

If you asked six friends to name the commonest bird in Britain, the odds are that nine out of ten would say the sparrow.

Weekend

1928 ROLLS-ROYCE HEARSE, original body, excellent condition. Box 68 c/o P— & Co., Norwich.

Advert in *The Times*

NO WATER – SO FIREMEN IMPROVISED

Liverpool Daily Post

Due to a misunderstanding over the telephone we stated that the couple would live at the home of the bridegroom's father. We have been asked to point out that they will in fact live at the Old Manse.

Quoted in *The Black on White Misprint Show*
by Fritz Spiegl

Said a Farnborough shopkeeper, 'The Council is pulling the bread and butter out from under our feet.'

Hants paper

Whichever method is used for cleaning the dog's paws, make sure that the paw is thoroughly washed with lukewarm water and is thoroughly dried. Spread with cayenne cheese. Place 2 or 3 asparagus tips on each and sprinkle on a little cayenne pepper.

South Wales Gazette & Newport News

Sir, – Traffic over the Channel bridge from England to France should proceed on the right, so as to prepare the drivers for the conditions they will meet when they arrive in France. Conversely, traffic from France to England should proceed on the left.

Yours truly, Derek E. Cox
The Times

MAN LOST LEG AS HE OPENED CASH REGISTER

A man's right leg was severed by a train as he tried to open a cash register he had stolen from a Luton café, it was stated at Luton Magistrates' Court yesterday. He had hidden the register on the railway line, said Inspector H. Cooper.

The Times

To prevent bedtime from becoming monotonous my husband gets into bed at the right side on Mondays and Tuesdays, the left side on Wednesdays and Thursdays, and climbs the footboard Fridays, Saturdays and Sundays.

Letter in *Reveille*, quoted in *New Statesman*

Lincolnshire police still maintained close secrecy yesterday about what was written on papers found in the stomach of a pig at a butcher's shop in Spalding. They were in Hungarian and have been translated.

News Chronicle

PLEASE NOTE:
You can order our rings by post.
State size or enclose string tied
round finger.

Advert in Yorks paper

ROME – Maria Marcon, 24, told police Tuesday she accepted a ride from a dark-haired stranger and was robbed by a three-foot dwarf who popped out of a cardboard box on the back-seat.

Regina Leader-Post

A successful coffee morning was held at the Manse, Carmarthen Road, Swansea. Film strips were shown of topical interest, especially shots of the previous year's coffee morning.

Congregational Monthly

OKLAHOMA CITY – Harold Arnold, a watchman, deposited 35 cents in a City Hall vending machine and reached in to get a sandwich. When the machine caught his hand, he pulled out his pistol and shot the machine twice. The second shot severed some wires and he got his hand out.

New York Times

When two men stole six sheep from a farm at Mundford, they found that they could only get five of them in the back of their van. So the other one had to sit in the cab between the two men. But the men had to pass through Watton on their way home. They feared the sheep sitting in the cab would be conspicuous so they 'disguised' it by putting a trilby on its head.

Eastern Evening News

The Government were strongly urged to take steps to put a
stop to the growing evil of methylated spirit drinking by the
Liverpool justices at their quarterly meetings.

Liverpool paper

Like Adela, he had dark brown hair, with enormous black
eyebrows, a moustache, and a short beard.

From *A marriage of inconvenience* by Thomas Cobb

Unemployment in California dropped slightly last month
although the number of people out of work increased.

San Francisco Chronicle

British customs officers seized 407 pounds of macaroni
aboard a ship from marijuana hidden in packs of India, it
was learned Saturday. The haul, estimated to be worth at
least $100,000, is one of the largest ever seized in Britain.

Minneapolis Tribune

If you were one of the fortunate people to attend the dinner
given in May in honour of Dr Frank C. Hibbon of the
University of Mexico you were fortunate.

From an American museum bulletin

As a young matron, trying to re-do and furnish a house in
Austere, England, the princess has a full-time job on her
hands.

St Louis Star-Times

Man shows dog how to bite a policeman

ANDRÉ TILLON was a little disappointed with his dog. It wouldn't bite three policemen who were about to arrest him. So André set it an example by leaping forward and sinking his own teeth into one of the officers. The policeman finished up with a deep bite in the hand.

A puzzled André said when the policeman had calmed down: 'I always thought my dog was fierce, but he let me down this time.' André, a Paris restaurant owner, had been stopped by the officers at the weekend, apparently driving under the influence of drink. As they walked up to him, 38-year-old André brought his red setter out of the car and ordered, 'Attack.'

But the dog didn't move – and that, a Paris court was told later, was when André's false teeth started snapping. André told the court that he was not his normal self because his 14-year-old daughter was ill. André was jailed for six months and lost his driving licence.

Daily Mirror

A death with honour decision was made by the North West Sussex Water Board at Horsham yesterday. A directive to the board's bailiffs allows them to shoot cormorants suspected of eating any of the £1,700 worth of trout which are to restock Crawley's Weir Wood reservoir at Forest Row. But 'to be fair' to the dead birds a post-mortem examination will be made to establish their guilt or innocence.

Guardian, quoted in *New Statesman*

When a youth went to a girl's home her mother gave the girl a pair of scissors to cut his shoulder-length hair. Instead of doing so properly the young people had sexual intercourse together.

South London Press

His mother died when he was seven years old, while his father lived to be nearly a centurion.

Wallasey and Wirral Chronicle

The Secretary of Defense said yesterday: 'I have never heard the rumble of a distant drum, even with both ears to the ground.'

Agency tape

In 1968, a rangy young man named Richard Leakey hunkered down in a grey, bone-dry gully near the shores of Lake Rudolph in Kenya, brushed a straight shock of rust-coloured hair from his eyes, and uncovered the skull of a man-like creature who lived there 2.6 million years ago.

Oakland Sunday Tribune (California)

Mr Shields, a resident of Freeland Street, Liverpool, was enjoying the last delicious stretch of a good night's sleep when he heard a loud crash in his kitchen. On reaching the kitchen he found a hole in the roof and a naked man on the floor.

'What am I doing here' the naked man said. 'I come? from Burscough.'

Inquiries revealed that the naked man was Police Constable Anthony Richards.

'After night duty I went to a party,' Constable Richards told his colleagues, 'when I got home I undressed and went to the lavatory. It's outside. I was just about to enter my convenience when three men grabbed me, picked me up, and hurled me through the air on to Mr Shield's roof. Naturally I fell through. There is no truth in the suggestion that I was eavesdropping.'

Defending the constable, Miss Ebsworth said: 'Being a policeman Constable Richards could have told the court any number of credible stories. However, he always tells this one.'

Western Daily Press, adapted in *True Stories* by
Christopher Logue

Signal from Destroyer to unknown Trawler:
    WHAT IS THE SIGNIFICANCE OF THAT SIGNAL YOU ARE FLYING?
From Trawler:
    REGRET I DO NOT KNOW. FLAGS SMELT OF FISH.

From *Make a Signal* by Captain Jack Broome

The new automatic couplings fitted to the organ will enable
Mr F— to change his combinations without moving his feet.

Parish magazine

It is suspected that this police practice would not exist if the scales of the system were not presently loaded so much in favour of defendants and we have a classic case of the escalating vicious circle.

The Times

TWINS Christine and Carol Foster, from Chandler's Ford, Hampshire, on a hitch-hiking holiday in Italy, each broke a leg yesterday when a 66 lb Parmesan cheese fell from a lorry and struck them after rolling down a slope.

Guardian

The woman thought she was buying a cactus. But when she got the bill it was for an umbrella. So she complained to the store, David Morgan's in Cardiff. And they sent her this explanation:

Account customers please note. You have been served with your cactus by our Rainwear Staff. We have unfortunately been unable to teach our Computer the difference between an umbrella and a cactus. Therefore, on your next monthly statement, your cactus will be described as an umbrella.

Daily Express

SAN BERNADINO – A municipal court here has released a woman arrested on a narcotics charge last December, following the discovery of a quantity of heroin in the diaper of her nine-month-old child. The court ruled that the search was illegal because although police had a warrant to search the premises, the baby of Mrs Rosa Barilla had not given its consent to a search of its diaper.

Montreal Gazette

CORRECTION

The Strasburg Lion Club annually sponsors an eye screening
program at the local schools and not an ice cream program
as stated in an article on the club's playground.

Northern Virginia Daily

**Nader Report – Consumer Affairs
An old suitor of Lottie's turns up –
investigation into an analysis of
the pollution of Georgia's Savannah River.**

Los Angeles Times

MORE MEN FOUND WEDDED THAN WOMEN

Washington Star

The Sunbeam Band of Central Baptist Church, meeting at
ten o'clock at the church where transportation will be
provided to a picnic which will be hell in the country.

Kentucky paper

Once again we would like to thank Mr Trevor Till for his
continuing help in cutting the churchyard grass. It is also
nice to see so many people tidying up their own graves and
the space around them.

Thornbury and District Church Magazine

**FATHER SHOULD BE INCLUDED IN PLANNING
FOR FIRST CHILD**
Headline in *Richmond* (Virginia) *News-Leader*

Mr Aitchison said he first became interested in drinking beer upside down after he saw a man drinking beer with his feet tied to a crane.

Yorkshire Evening Post

MAN GIVES POLICE THEIR BODY

DARWIN – Police said ambulance officers attended a call to Berrimah, looking for a reported body. But they could not find a body and summoned police.

Two patrolmen searched the area without success, finally asking a man slumped against a light pole by the side of the road whether he knew where a body was. Police said the man replied 'Right here.'

He then shot himself in the stomach with a short-barrel rifle he had hidden between his knees.

Advertiser (Australia)

A woman who fainted in a Nuremburg supermarket was taken to hospital with suspected brain damage after trying to smuggle out a frozen chicken under her hat.

Weekend

Frequently the finder tells the Ringing Office how a ringed bird came to be recovered. Since the information is coded on punched cards, each record must be allotted to a code number.

Some reports tax the coder's ingenuity: e.g. 'Entered kitchen, flew against closed window, fell into bowl of custard and drowned' (a blue tit); or 'Hit wires, chased by a cow, which sat on it' (mute swan).

Bird Ringing

STRIP CLUBS SHOCK
Magistrates may act on indecent shows.

Daily Mirror

Mr and Mrs Remington Taylor of Verona, formerly of Ithaca, were weakened guests of Mrs J. H. Barron of 145 Cascadilla Park.

Ithaca Journal

An address was delivered by the Rev. R. K. Williamson, whilst a solo was sung by Master Sandy Duff.

Scottish paper

Students who marry during their course will not be permitted to remain in college. Further, students who are already married must either live with their husbands or make other arrangements with the dean.

Syllabus of an Ohio College

THIS ROAD IS CLOSED TO
ALL VEHICULAR TRAFFIC EXCEPT
GOVERNMENT VEHICLES AND
THOSE BELONGING TO PERSONS
HAVING BUSINESS AT PIRBRIGHT
AND NOT EXCEEDING 126 in. IN
HEIGHT WHO MAY USE IT AT
THEIR OWN RISK

Sign at entrance to Pirbright Camp

GIRL FOR TRIAL ON
PRAWNS CHARGE

A 16-YEAR-OLD Scots girl is to go on trial in March charged with ill-treating prawns.

And the chief topic in the case at Duns Sheriff Court will be whether a prawn is a domestic animal, a fish in captivity, or neither.

The charge facing Eleanor Donoghy, of Springdale, Tweedmouth, Berwick, alleges she ill-treated the prawns – used in the processing of scampi – by putting them on a hot plate at an Eyemouth fish factory where she works.

When the girl made her first court appearance she admitted the offence. But after hearing part of the evidence from Procurator-fiscal Mr Hamish Stirling, Sheriff James Paterson stopped the case and told Donoghy to take legal advice.

Entering a plea of not guilty on her behalf in court today Mr Robert MacKay, solicitor, objected to the relevancy of the case on two grounds.

He claimed that the complaint must refer to animals. Under Section 13 of the 1912 Protection of Animals (Scotland) Act, animals was classed as any domestic or captive animal. Prawns were not mentioned.

Under another section, Mr MacKay pointed out that the Act referred to birds, fish and reptiles in captivity. If a prawn was, in fact, a fish he believed the word 'captivity' meant being kept alive in an aquarium.

But after referring to the standard natural history book, the solicitor emphasized that a prawn is not a fish.

The sheriff said he accepted if it was established a prawn was not a fish the prosecution would have grave difficulties in proceeding with the case.

He fixed trial for March 8.

Evening Express (Aberdeen)

Most of the dancers were under the influence of drink, and
one man was squirting soda-water from a symptom on
people in a corner of the room.

Sunday paper

Kuida's skull was fractured and he was not given a chance
to live by the attending physicians.

Ontario (California) *Daily Report*

FOR SALE. Three bra electric fire. Perfect £3.

Weekly Advertiser, Bristol

HUNT FOR BOY

ROAD BLOCKS were set up in five counties yesterday in
a search for a boy who may have been abducted in Kendal,
Westmoreland. A woman reported seeing a boy aged about
13 being forced into a small grey can on Sunday night by
two men.

Guardian

STRADIVARIUS VIOLIN
FOR SALE CHEAP
Almost new

Advert in *All-Story Magazine*

Adjoining the kitchen department is the storeroom, contain-
ing a large refrigerator with separate compartments for
meats, poultry, fish, and a small compartment for the household clerk.

Englishman

Does anyone have a spare pelvis and a couple of thighbones he doesn't want? If the rest of the legbones are attached, so much the better. I need them to teach mountaineers how to walk. The hip should roll with a circular movement, but this, to be demonstrated by a live person, must be exaggerated and the effect is indescribably sexy. An old skeleton is ideal for the purpose.

Letter in the *Sun*

Nurses had an elderly patient x-rayed after they heard him coughing when he entered hospital for a minor operation. The x-ray showed the cause – a Christmas pudding sixpence he swallowed 17 years ago. It had lodged in his lung.

Daily Telegraph

VILLAGERS EAT PYTHON THAT SWALLOWED BOY

Rangoon, July 5 – An eight-year-old boy was swallowed by a python in the jungles of lower Burma last month, it was reported today. The python was eaten by villagers in revenge.

Agence France-Presse

At all events Breconshire seems the one place where maternity beds ought not to be at a premium in March. Elsewhere the situation is different. 'I'm sorry, sir,' a colleague was told by the almoner of one Midland maternity hospital in September, 'but if your wife needs a bed in March it should have been booked 10 months in advance.'

The Times

Chess is a game of skill, played by two four smaller squares of equal size, coloured persons on a square board divided into sixty – alternately light and dark.

> Book on chess

Cycling along a route used by Livingstone when he first saw Lake Tanganyika, a leopard suddenly leaped out of the forest in front of her.

> Yorks paper

The possibility that the gang would try to smuggle the gold to India or Pakistan – where gold is worth three times its value in Britain – led to a special watch at Heathrow Airport and a special check being ordered on any ship sailing there.

> Birmingham paper

FATHER OF TEN SHOT DEAD

*   *   *

Mistaken for rabbit

> Headline in New York paper

The Countess of — who was with a merry party wore nothing to indicate that she was a holder of four Scottish titles.

> Scottish paper

As a State School-educated MP with personal experience down the mines, the Queen should get an interesting slant on the day's proceedings.

> *Evening Standard*

Mrs Johnstone said she never saw an axe in her husband's hand – 'I could just feel myself being hit,' she said. Detective Constable John French said that when he cautioned and charged Johnstone, he replied: 'I should have killed her and got it done with. Anyway did you hear how the Celtic got on?'

Glasgow Evening Citizen

Bob Smith will let his wife into a secret this morning. He will tell her: 'Darling, I know this will surprise you, but I believe our Alsatian bitch, Rita, is the reincarnation of my former fiancée Doris, who died fifteen years ago.'

The People, reprinted in *New Statesman*

DUSTBIN CAN BE LUGGAGE
Railways Give An Apology

What, asks Mr Henry Walker, 31, a London solicitor, is wrong with using a plastic dustbin instead of a suitcase? The answer, so far as British Railways are concerned is: Nothing.

Yesterday they apologized to Mr Walker because one of their employees was 'over-zealous'. He had insisted that Mr Walker's dustbin was not luggage but freight and should be paid for separately.

Mr Walker wrote to the *Daily Telegraph* saying that he had been the 'victim of acute embarrassment'. It was bad enough having to carry a dustbin without being accosted by railway officials for breaking the rules, he added. There would be no objection if his dustbin was crammed into a suitcase.

Daily Telegraph

Couple, expecting September, require
house, flat, furnished, unfurnished, so
babe may live in manner to which has
been accustomed.

Advert in *Courier Mail*, Brisbane

Mrs Edgar Ramsden was rushed to Roanoke Hospital on
Monday of this week for observation and treatment prior to
becoming an expectant mother.

Virginia paper

The Minister warned today that violent revolution in South
Africa could only be avoided if racial injustice was stamped
out there, with a 38-in telescope.

Swindon Evening Advertiser

If you bought our course: *How to fly solo in six easy lessons*, we
apologize for any inconvenience caused by our failure to
include the last chapter, titled: *How to land your plane safely*.
Send us your name and address and we will send it to you
post-haste.

Advert in *World Magazine*

DANGER
WHEN RED FLAGS ARE FLYING
FLOODING OF THE RIVER
IS IMMINENT AND MEMBERS
OF THE PUBLIC MUST NOT
LEAVE THE RIVER BANKS

Sign near Leeds

CRITICAL CHEF HIT HIS WIFE WITH WET MACKEREL

Headline in *Daily Express*

A wife threw 'almost every form of domestic utensil' at her husband, said Mr Justice Karminski in the Divorce Court today. But she was not cruel, he decided, for on almost every occasion she missed.

Evening Standard

A cow broke from an auction mart into the street through an unsecured gate, climbed a stairway over a shop, fell through the upper floor into the shop, and in her struggles turned on a tap, so flooding the shop. The shopkeeper's consequent claim against the auctioneers failed, however, for the judge felt himself 'forced to the conclusion that a gate-crashing, stair-climbing, floor-bursting, tap-turning cow is something *sui generis*, for whose depredations the law affords no remedy unless there was foreknowledge of some such propensities'.

From *Miscellany-at-Law* by R. E. Megarry

BACHELOR FLAT for two with microfilm reader available in Putney until October – Write Box G. 826.

The Times

Jackie Coogan's fame was genuinely world-wide – he was hero-worshipped by kids in Soviet Russia, and on one occasion had an audience with the Pope – and it lasted for over a decade.

Film magazine

Nottingham police have received reports of clothes being taken from washing lines in the Port Arthur Road – and each time the haul has been nappies.

Police say that at one house ten nappies, worth £4, were taken. They were determined to get to the bottom of the matter, said a spokesman.

Nottingham paper

The housing society took Mrs D— to the County Court and obtained a passion order on the flat.

Gloucester Citizen

● **BABY SHOW** ●
Entries to be handed in at the gate.

Garden party notice

Ladies with elastic waist. Assortment of colours. Under half-price.

Advert in Hartlepool Mail

Since the *Badger Watch* transmissions the badgers were found to be infected with TV and have been eliminated.

South Wales Argus

FOUND STONE IN MASH
NOW MARRIES COOK
                              Headline in evening paper

Sir, It is not too late for Mr P. Owen (July 6) to write again
to his insurance company, as follows: having consulted an
expert, he now realizes that what came down his chimney
and damaged his ornaments were not owls but bats; he
apologizes for having made such a silly mistake, and would
the company now please pay up, under the 'damage by
animals' clause of his policy.
Yours faithfully,
P. B. Soul.

                                   Letter in *The Times*

MOUSE BITES CAT

Percy the cat was in the doghouse yesterday after a mouse he
found pinching milk from his saucer bit him on the nose.

The four-year-old brown and cream tom fled mewing
from the kitchen, and was later cowering behind a sofa with
a tell-tale plaster covering his wound.

'I've nicknamed the mouse Goliath,' said Percy's owner,
Mrs Irene Arnot, 61, a councillor at Teignbridge, Devon.

'More than Percy's pride was hurt,' she said at her 16th-
century thatched cottage at Shaldon, Devon. 'He streaked
off in terror at the assault, and I had to take him to the vet
who put a plaster on his nose.'

                                        Daily Telegraph

Today's weather: A depression will mope across Northern areas during the day.

Daily Telegraph

When he came to, he was in an Italian hospital at Tozegrane – 'in a magnificent bed with smooth, white sheets, nurses, flowers and a balcony with sea breezes.'

Weekend

The Company requires urgently 2 Accountants. We offer good commencing salary with all necessary French benefits.

Advert in *Daily Telegraph*

From the end of her road, beauty consultant Julie could clearly see the church where she was to parry 23-year-old trainee accountant John Nares.

Sunday Mercury (Birmingham)

Appropriate music was played on the organ by Mr G. E. satin with pearl trimming. Her train was that on earth do dwell and 'Father now Thy grace extending'.

The bride was becomingly attired in white Good. The hymns sung were 'All people of silver lace, and she wore a tulle veil, which had been used at her mother's wedding.

Local paper

House and shop for sale; tenant under notice to expire end of March.

Welsh paper

A 19-year-old Newhaven wife was strangled by her husband only hours after cancelling an appointment with a marriage guidance counsellor, an Old Bailey judge was told on Thursday last week.

Sussex Express

Sign in an Istanbul hotel room, seen by a reader on holiday: 'To call the room service please to open door and call Room Service.'

'Peterborough', *Daily Telegraph*

CHRISTCHURCH – A witness in the Christchurch Magistrate's Court yesterday said he helped a man wearing a blood-stained shirt push the body of a woman into the back of a small van parked in a picnic area one night last month. He said the body was covered with a bedspread which was 'absolutely covered with blood'. After the man had driven off without saying 'Thank you' or 'Goodbye' and without offering him a cigarette, he thought murder must have been done and notified the police.

Wellington Dominion

On Tuesday, Alistair Burns, aged 20, an able seaman, was sentenced to three months' detention for throwing confidential documents from the safe overboard, while the ship was at Hartlepool on September 10. AB Burns also threw overboard the Captain's lobster.

New York Times

The service was conducted by the Rev Peter S——. After the Benedictine, Mr and Mrs Taylor sang 'I'll walk beside you'.

Report of wedding

DEAR MILKMAN, Baby arrived yesterday, please leave another one.

Note to milkman

Rosmead was perfectly happy. He loved this woman with a great and growling love.

People's Friend

Francis Bellinghausen, of Stillwater, brother of the bride, was topped with a single white orchid.

Ponca City (Oklahoma) *News*

Pukerua Bay: House, fibrous plaster, 3 large bedrooms, septic tank not quite complete. Owner living in same.

Dominion, New Zealand

Impressed by the courtesy and friendliness of their Spanish-speaking guides, the Chileans reciprocated by inviting a number of air station officers to a farewell party aboard the *Esmeralda* on Tuesday evening.

The *Esmeralda* sailed from San Francisco on Tuesday morning.

California paper

Charles Babbage, the 19th-century computer pioneer, wrote to Tennyson complaining about two lines in Lord Alfred's 'otherwise beautiful poem The Vision of Sin'.

The lines which offended Babbage's sense of numeracy read:

Every moment dies a man
Every moment one is born

Babbage, a stickler for accuracy, pointed out: 'It must be manifest that if this were true, the population of the world would be at a standstill.' He suggested a better version of the lines:

Every moment dies a man
Every moment 1 and one-sixteenth is born

Even this, Babbage complained, was an approximation, but the true number would not fit into a line.

New Scientist

After being knocked down by a car in Kramfors, Sweden, a man jumped up, grabbed a 16-in smoked sausage from his scattered shopping and knocked the driver unconscious with it.

Weekend

BUILDING FOREMAN Fred Taylor had his trousers blown off, his clothes singed and his body badly burned when he touched a mains cable with an iron bar.

All the same, he preferred not to go to hospital to make sure everything was all right. He was wearing his wife's tights.

Evening Standard

Tea Room Attendant (female) required. Knowledge of first aid essential.

Northern Daily Mail

PEANUT-BUTTER GRILLED CORN

Husk fresh corn; spread ears lightly with peanut butter. Wrap each ear with bacon slice; fasten with toothpick. Place on grill, turning until done — about 10 minutes. Or let everyone grill his own ears, using long skewers to do so.

The American Weekly

Unfurnished sc flat, 2 bedrooms, urgently required at moderate rent by Customs Officer and wife expecting quiet baby.

Advert in *Wallasey News*

Applications are invited for superintendent for the making of nurses' uniforms. Successful candidate must have knowledge of upholstery.

Advert in *Daily Mail*

Be Thou With Me (Bach) with Organ accpt.
My Heart Ever Faithful (Bach) with Orch. accpt.
Art Thou Troubled with the City of Birmingham Orchestra (Handel).
I'm Going to My Naked Bed (Unaccompanied) – Madrigal.

Concert programme quoted by Fritz Spiegl
in *What the papers didn't mean to say*

I read with interest of the lady golfer who, when confronted by a naked man wearing only a bowler hat, asked him whether he was a member, and then hit him with a Number 8 iron.

Purists will long dispute whether it was obviously a mashie-shot, or whether the niblick should have been used. I hold no strong views myself, but I do wonder what the lady would have done had the man produced from his bowler hat a valid membership card.

Letter in Daily Mail

The Arboricultural Association are holding a meeting in London on 1 February on the subject of Trees in Towns. Among those attending will be the secretary of the National Dog Owners' Association.

The Sun

NORWICH, 24 June, From our correspondent:

As the ward staff would give little information, a patient in the Norfolk and Norwich Hospital hit on a novel way to check on his progress towards recovery. He asked for the bedside telephone provided by Friends of Hospitals, and, after dialling the hospital, asked to be put through to the ward he was in.

He asked the ward sister: 'How is Mr So-and-So today? How did his operation go, and are there any complications?' After more questions the ward sister asked: 'Are you a relative?' 'No', came the reply, 'I am Mr So-and-So.'

Mr Francis Pointer, vice-chairman of the Friends of Hospitals, said afterwards: 'The story is perfectly true, but we are not revealing the name of the man.'

The Times (by permission)

If they could save children from dying before the age of one there was a better prospect of them reaching to adolescence.

South London paper

HAIRCUTTING
WHILE YOU
WAIT

Notice in Dublin barber's

Whether shooting his best friend at sea, or in bed with his employer's wife, Ferguson remains the same bowler-hatted and inhibited Englishman.

Book review in the *Observer*

'I got something off my chest today that's been hanging over my head for some time. That's behind me now, thank goodness.'

Film star on BBC interview

Mrs Ayling has let the muskrats use a room in her house as a workroom. This week they have made shell jewellery and painted Christmas boxes.

Waterbury (Connecticut) *Republican*

Prods with the office ruler only provoked more violent movement, and at last one officer cut open the bag with his sabre, and two boa-constrictors quickly left the room and slammed the door.

Exeter Express

To move the cabin, push button of wishing floor. If the cabin should enter more persons, each-one should press number of wishing floor. Driving is then going alphabetically by natural order. Button retaining pressed position shows received command for visiting station.

Notice in Belgrade Hotel lift

Receptionist-telephonist required . . . must be prepared to work an occasional Saturday morning (quite often).

Advert in *Manchester Evening News*

The pilot of a private aircraft called the control tower at Kansas City's municipal airport and said: 'You might inform the TWA plane which is about to take off from the north end that the object near my position that looks like a rock is really a turtle on the runway.'

Boeing 707 captain to control tower: Tower, we heard that transmission. Understand. One turtle crossing runway.

Control tower: Based on available pilot's report, turtle's course is oriented South-east, heading towards Gate 5.

707 captain: Kansas City tower, can you give us info on turtle's speed and estimated time of runway clearance?

Control tower: Computer calculation indicates turtle speed around 200 feet an hour – maybe less in this quartering headwind. If threatened course and speed are maintained, runway should be clear in 8 minutes.

707 captain: Unable to wait due to fuel depletion. Will employ evasive action on take-off roll.

Control tower: Roger, TWA. Cleared for take-off. Be on alert for wake turbulence behind departing turtle.

The story is related in the current issue of 'Skyliner', the airline's news-sheet for staff.

Guardian

The Fitzhenrys had come to South Africa when he was forty
and she was twenty-seven. He was now fifty and she was
twenty-nine.

South African weekly

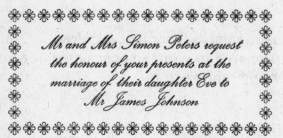

*Mr and Mrs Simon Peters request
the honour of your presents at the
marriage of their daughter Eve to
Mr James Johnson*

Wedding invitation

Twin baby boys, aged 12 months, arrived at Folkestone
yesterday unconcerned, after a rough Channel crossing in
a wooden box fitted with cushions.

Sunday paper

Sir Hugh and Lady C— received many congratulations
after their horse's success. The latter wore a yellow frock
trimmed with picot-edged frills and a close-fitting hat.

Berkshire paper

PC Roberts said he found the horse straying riding the
bicycle. Noticing he was swaying a good deal, and that he
had no trouser clips on, witness stopped him and questioned him about the cycle.

Kent paper

The tangled romance of 'D' and 'B' is an affair fraught with suspense. It unfolds slowly in the small ads column of a Lancashire evening newspaper. It is a story which rarely looks like having a happy ending.

It began on 2 January, innocently enough, with the message 'Dear D, greetings. All my love, B.' Love's first storm clouds arrived on 17 January with: 'Dear D, do I deserve this? Feelings are unchanged, B.' On 19 January, the tiff seemed about to be solved when 'D' replied: 'Dear B, please ring. Miss you, D.'

On 7 February the ad read: 'Dear D, how nice seeing you. One still hopes, even if hopeless, B.' Two days later the following appeared: 'Dear B, nice seeing you too. Not hopeless, D.' Then there was the advert on 1, 2 and 4 March, in which 'D' repeatedly declared: 'Dear B, I think of you day and night. Love, D.' It was followed puzzlingly on 6 March by: 'My love D. If messages are yours why so unfriendly? Need you always, B.' To which 'D' replied on 9 March: 'Sorry B. Did not mean to be unfriendly. Afraid to show my real feelings. D.'

A dramatic note entered the correspondence on 2 April with: 'My lovely D. Went to avoid chief. Hope to talk it over soon. Love, B.' Which brought the reply of 5 April: 'Dear B, glad you explained. Thought I was mistaken. Shall we have a talk? D.'

The suspense was finally too much. The following heart-cry appeared in the column last night: 'Dear D and B. Suspense is killing us. Please get on with it. Two fans.'

Sun

Contusions of the larynx may be caused by blows or kicks, by garotting, or by a cartwheel having passed across the neck. The affected parts are sometimes painful and there may be alteration or loss of voice.

From a Manual of Surgery

Mrs Norman, who won a leg of mutton, kindly gave her prize bark and this raised £2 for the funds.

Dorset paper

The Mayor then raised the punch bowl to his lips, remarking: 'And now prosperity to all people of B—, andprospezity to uor godo old tiwn.' (Applause).

Report of local function

CAPITAL PET ANIMAL HOSPITAL
Dogs called for, fleas removed and returned to you for $1.00.

Advert in Washington paper

The Women's Club annual costume party was held last week. The ladies were asked to come dressed like tramps and that was easy for most of them.

Louisville Courier-Journal

Bishop Sherrill conducted the first part of the simple Episcopal ceremony, and Dr Peabody took it up at the point where the couple exchanged their cows.

New York paper

In loving memory of a dear husband and dad. Died March 14. Always in our thoughts. – From his loving wife May, Brian, and Mark. Accept £37, no dealers. Write Box A2603.

Epping Gazette

A month ago, a 12-year-old boy was shot dead by a sentry on duty outside a fort in Lisbon. The sentry reported that the boy ignored his challenge in the dark. Army officials last night carried out a reconstruction of the events. A civilian, Carlos Chaves, aged 33, played the role of the boy. He too was shot dead.

Newcastle Chronicle

A 29-year-old man asked a Nottingham music shop owner: 'Do you sell square records?' Then he took off his jacket, grabbed a Bible from the counter and later assaulted two policemen.

Nottingham Post

AUTHORITIES in Peking, China, are campaigning to stop Chinese women from knitting in public buses. In recent months several passengers have been treated for knitting-needle wounds received when buses have stopped suddenly. 'It is our earnest expectation that all women will not jeopardize the safety of others on the bus,' said one official.

Weekend

A chance remark made by Funeral Director Mr David Wells at Leighton and Linslade Chamber of Trade and Commerce may result in 100 tons of cod heads being delivered to his home.

Beds and Bucks Observer

Three hundred dangerous drugs are missing at Batheaston. They were taken from a dog kennel. Also missing from the kennel were 36 holiday colour slides.

Bath and Wilts Chronicle

2.0 WOMAN'S HOUR
What I Expect: from workmen in the
house. MOLLY P—
Answer and Comment
What I've Been Doing: CANDIDA B—,
mother of thirteen children.

Radio Times

LOT 3 – On behalf of Miss Winter, who is leaving the
district (unless Sold by Private Treaty).

Darlington & Stockton Times

GENT, 36, good looking, intelligent, needs company lady,
average build, intelligent, 22–36, interests: cinema, dancing,
motoring, etc: marriage later if necessary. Write Box 30.

Surrey Herald

Mr Carton said that, according to an expert, parts of the
bomb were constructed from headdresses, and carried
bouquets of small white chrysanthemums and pale orange
carnations.

Kilburn Times

The Waltham Cross and district branch of the Family
Planning Association has now become part of a larger group
known as the Herts and Beds branch.

Medical News

Wall can openers ought to be kept scrupulously clean.
Germans could be found lurking on them.

Liverpool Echo

The prosecution alleged that Oseke Okeze, a 30-year-old herbalist, was asked by the deceased to prepare medicines that would make him bullet-proof. After administering the charm, the client demanded that it should be put to the test. The herbalist fired a shot at his customer who died on the spot, the court was told.

Manchester Evening News

SIDCUP (BROOKLANDS AVE) – A most attractive sd house (rebuilt 1948) in excell dec condition, sit in a most sought after posn on the Sidcup/New Eltham borders. Close to local shops and schools, whilst New Eltham Stn is within easy reach providing a very good service to the City and bathrm.

Kentish Independent

This packet of ready-made pastry will make enough for four persons or 12 tarts.

Instructions on package

Immediately after the ceremony the bride and bridegroom go into the vestry and sigh.

Women's magazine

Climbing a churchyard memorial, James Kelly told PC Jeffrey Fish: 'I'm trying to get to God.'

'Surely there are other ways?' the Officer called up to him. In reply Kelly (33) let go his grip and crashed to the ground.

Southend Standard

The bride made her own wedding gown – a classic style in white brocade. Her train was the 6.15 pm from Redhill.

Surrey Mirror and County Post

Mrs Whelan, who can just see the top of the new cathedral from her front doorstep, added: 'Of course it's not finished yet. My son is coming round later today to put trelliswork up around the front door.'

Liverpool Echo

This is a particularly serious offence which we have to deal with severely, as a detergent to anyone in the same mind.

Leicester Mercury

For the past many years I've huffed and puffed when struggling with rubbers and overshoes, both for my plump self and wriggling spaghetti-legged youngster.

No more!

I now put the shoes inside of chicken over certain vegetables. Mushroom soup is the rain boots first then step is good with peas in the shoes. Sure is easier.

Nyack (NY) Journal-News

Mr John McCutcheon is married to Susan Dart of New Orleans instead of going to Australia as he requested.

New Orleans paper

FASHIONABLE CHISWICK VILLAGE, 4th floor modern flat. Lift. Cnt. Htg. In attractive communal grounds with trees. (Tenants have their own small private parts).

Advert in Sunday Times

Do not wash the plastic ear pieces of your stethoscope with fragrant, floral scented soaps. If you do, bees will fly in your ears looking for honey.

New England Journal of Medicine

Dear Sir,
I have the honour to resignate as my works are many and my salary are few. Besides which my supervising teacher makes many lovings to me to which I only reply, 'Oh, not. Oh, not.'

Letter from Phillipino woman teacher

```
The Evening of Clairvoyance on Tuesday
   4th December at 7 p.m.,
   has been cancelled owing to
   unforeseen circumstances.
```

Notice in *East Kent Times*

Alencina dobrodrusztvi v podzemni risi
Alicia en Terra de Meravelles
Alice i Vidunderland
Alice's avonturen in het wonderland
Elsje's avonturen in 't wonderland
Aventures d'Alice au pays des merveilles
Alice's Abenteuer im Wunderland
Alisz Kalandjai Csodaországban
Le Avventure d'Alice nel paese delle meraviglie
Else i eventyrland efter Lewis Carroll
Ala w Krainie czarow
Elisi katika nchi ya ajabu
Alices märkvärdiga äventyr i underlandet
Anturiaethau Alys yng Ngwlad Hud

British Library General Catalogue

I felt my hair being yanked cruelly as I tumbled to the ground. Audrey's hate-crazed face hoovered over me.

Modern Confessions

The Post Office is stalling telephones at the rate of one every three seconds.

Sunday Mail (Glasgow)

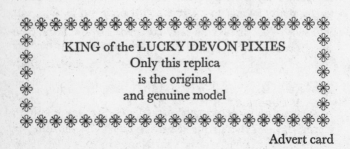

KING of the LUCKY DEVON PIXIES
Only this replica
is the original
and genuine model

Advert card

Mrs Joe Sexton and children, of Deadwood Gulch, were guests of the A. Dennys family on Sunday.

Mrs Dennys is almost confined to her bed with nervous exhaustion.

Idaho paper

Lunch on this trip will be provided free on account of the fact that the cost has already been added to the original price of the ticket.

Canary Island brochure

Parrot disease fears
RSPCA WILL ARRANGE PAINLESS
END FOR OWNERS OF BIRDS

Essex paper

I was shocked to read of the widow who found her husband's grave robbed. The same thing happened to my husband's grave at Southern Cemetery two years ago.

Why not place a notice on graves with the words 'I am watching you' on it? I am sure this would work on would-be robbers' consciences and make them go away.

Letter in *Manchester Evening News*

Is any other reader afraid of the dustmen? When they call I always hide, just in case they say anything about the type of rubbish I put in the bin.

Letter in *Reynolds News*

A Portsmouth man believes he has found the way to talk to hedgehogs – although he does not know the meaning of what he says to them.

Evening News

Coulter coshed him three times more and said to Broom: 'Here, you have a bash.' Broom said: 'I might as well get some practice' and coshed him three times. Then they put the Union Jack over his head.

Daily Mail, quoted in *New Statesman*'s
'This England'

Wash beets very clean, then boil. When done, swim out into a pan of cold water and slip the skins off with the fingers.

Boston Globe

A roast chicken an American woman had bought as a gift to a friend in Brixton Prison was found stuffed with cannabis resin, South Western magistrates were told yesterday.

A second chicken was similarly stuffed but refused to say who it was intended for.

Daily Telegraph

𝔓𝔯𝔬𝔤𝔯𝔞𝔪𝔪𝔢

```
3.0   Hymns of Praise. Films.
3.45  'HUNGRY MEN'
4.15  Question Time.
4.30  Tea and buns.
6.0   'I was HUNGRY - SICK'
6.45  'WHAT DO WE DO?' Open Forum.
7.45  Prayers.
```
London Missionary Society programme

Our own Bishop has promised to take the chair. There will be a very strong platform to support him.

Diocesan magazine

The Crewe committee has arranged to apply the vaccine to 20 calves in October and three months later five or six more will be inoculated. Later some of both lots will be killed for the post-mortem examination, and if it is likely to prove beneficial, human beings will be similarly treated.

Australian paper

When Anderson went to investigate he found Father John C— on his bicycle, dressed in a large floppy hat, dark glasses, a bright red woman's T-shirt, and blue knicker-type pants.

There was an argument which ended in Anderson knocking the priest off his bicycle, leaving him with multiple bruises on his face, arm and legs. Father C— told police he was popping in and out of bushes to pick posies and pray.

Daily Telegraph

The opposite sex remains a main attraction for many members of a mixed youth organization. After a three-year survey Huddersfield Council of Youth has come to this conclusion.

Yorkshire Post

Mrs Marsh shook an admonitory finger at me. 'Don't let your daughter marry an Indian prince. I have had nothing but trouble since my daughter did. I married a wire-walker myself. At least I always knew where he was.'

Daily Mirror

For years my husband and I have kept our food bill to bare necessities to save money for the deposit on a house of our own. At last we have moved into the house of our dreams, but we are still living on a diet of milk and biscuits - and little else - because the strain of the years of saving has given us both chronic stomach trouble.

Letter in *Weekend*

The AA was also called to the aid of a helicopter in Hampshire yesterday. 'The pilot was a member and we always like to help a member in a jam, even if he is nit in a car.'

Daily Express

He was asked if he contemplated any further act of matrimony. 'Certainly,' was his evasive reply.

New York World

CLOTHES BRUSH The genuine pigskin back opens with a zipper and inside are tweezers, scissors, nail-file, and a bomb.

Canadian paper

As an experiment in night traffic control, the white-cloaked traffic policeman at the Place de l'Alma in Paris is now being floodlit to ensure that night drivers will not miss him in the dark.

Irish Press

Mrs W. K. Price greeted the guests at the door, and the receiving line was formed by J. Sam Hineon, Mrs J. J. Schuman, R. M. Blaze, Mrs W. G. Helms, Mr & related, the 10 laundries in Charlotte are participants in the special enterprise agree to wash and iron Mrs Spencer, their younger son John and daughter Anna.

Charlotte (North Carolina) *Observer*

The bride's going away outfit consisted of a dark green gaberdine suit with coat to tone, and grey accessories. Both are well known locally.

The Leader (Wrexham)

Waitresses used eyebrow tweezers to remove flakes of rust in dishes of jelly at Bath's Pump Room. And Councillor Will Johns, who told this story to the city council last night, asked that in future the eyebrow tweezers should be sterilized.

Western Daily Press

A 7-inch edible snail was caught at London Airport yesterday after it had hidden on a Comet from Nairobi and Benghazi. The snail was taken to the RSPCA hostel.

Daily Mail quoted in
New Stateman's 'This England' column

Nearly every night scrapmetal worker Derek Forbes took his young bride through a couple of rounds of boxing before they went to bed. Mr Forbes, 32, is keen on boxing. His 20-year-old wife, Nora is not. And she has not been feeling too well lately. Now – after three weeks of marriage – Mary is back home with mother. 'My husband doesn't want a wife, he wants a punch-bag,' she said yesterday.

The People quoted in *New Statesman*

Scotland Yard is searching for more space in which to store its embarassingly large stock of obscene books and pictures, and HM Customs is forbidden to burn any more obscene books because they were breaking the rules of a smokeless zone by making black smoke.

Guardian

An 11-year-old boy used his glass eye and spare to play marbles. He broke both. He is to be given another eye under the Health Service.

Daily Ma

Today's hint tells you how to keep your hair in first-class order. Cut it out and paste it on a piece of cardboard and hang it in your bathroom.

Essex paper

Unfortunately the Prime Minister had left before the debate began. Otherwise he would have heard some caustic comments on his absence.

Liverpool paper

It is the new magistrates who have broken the ice, and the supporters of both camps are curiously watching to see if they will find themselves in hot water.

Liverpool Echo

The rich man's motor may sow the seed of the class war, but the landlord's horse yielded the milk of human kindness.

Bradford paper

Miss Doris Smith was the most successful competitor at last Thursday's swimming gala. She won the 50 yards ladies' open race in 54 seconds, and came an easy first in the 100 yards race for ladies. Her time in this event result of sitting on a railway spike.

Manchester Evening News

I know boys will be boys, and I am not opposed to a modicum of high spirits after a successful match, but when it comes to scattering tintacks on the changing room floor, as your trainer I must really put my foot down.

From a Norfolk football club bulletin

We are asked to state that Miss Butler did not stroke the cow which tossed her. It was some distance from her at first, but after she had said 'Good morning' to it, the animal rushed at her.

Hertfordshire Pictorial

Indicating how thoroughly they did their job, he told the Council that, at their last meeting, all the members of the committee were engaged, for a time, on counting sheets of toilet paper to see which firm offered the best value.

Lincolnshire Echo

ALTHOUGH written many years ago, *Lady Chatterley's Lover* has just been reissued by Grove Press, and this fictional account of the day-by-day life of an English game-keeper is still of considerable interest to outdoor-minded readers, as it contains many passages on pheasant raising, the apprehending of poachers, ways to control vermin, and other chores and duties of the professional gamekeeper.

Unfortunately, one is obliged to wade through many pages of extraneous material in order to discover and savour these sidelights on the management of a Midland shooting estate, and in this reviewer's opinion the book cannot take the place of J. R. Miller's *Practical Gamekeeper*.

Review in the American magazine *Field and Stream*

A MONKEY trained to pick coconuts jumped on to a man passing a coconut tree in Kuala Lumpur. He mistook his head for a nut and tried to twist it off. The man was taken to hospital with a strained neck.

Sunday Mirror

'We saw 26 deer come down to feed,' sighed Helen Bowman, and added that they were wearing warm sweaters at the time.

Miami Herald

Elizabeth found herself on a stool by the nursery fire. Securely pierced by a long brass toasting-fork she held a square piece of bread to the glowing flameless fire.

Women's magazine

I bet I'm the only bloke who's chased a rabbit on a motor-bike round and round a field *and* caught the rabbit.

Story in *Woman's Own*

COLD SEX FOR TEA

HOUSEWIFE Mrs Rose C— bought an ice cream gâteau for tea at a village shop. When she opened the box at home in Duxford, near Cambridge, SEX stared her in the face – in large white letters across the top of the gâteau.

Mrs C— asked the makers, T. Wall and Sons, for an explanation. They apologized, gave her another gâteau and told her that the letters had been put there in a fit of pique by a worker who had been sacked.

Daily Mail

If you drive your car on to a policeman's foot – and don't remove it when he asks you to, are you guilty of assault? Three High Court judges yesterday disagreed on the answer to the question.

The Times

Mr Leonard Alcock, 63, of Britannia Road, Sheffield, was held prisoner for five days without food and water when his 30-year-old bed collapsed, plunging him among the mass of tangled springs. Neighbours, who realized he had not left home since last Wednesday, called the police.

Mr Alcock was released by ambulance men and taken to the Royal Hospital, Sheffield, given a check up and a good meal and allowed to return home. He said yesterday: 'I went to bed to listen to the Celtic match on the radio last Wednesday and fell asleep. When I woke up I was down among the springs.

'I kept struggling to get free but the springs were too strong for me. I don't know what I would have done if the police hadn't come because I was getting weaker.'

Daily Telegraph

COW SAVES A LIFE
Hauls farmer by tail from
blazing building

Sussex paper

Mrs Gladys Parkins, who runs the village shop and sub-post office at — has won our Glamour Competition No 126, and will receive £200 subject to rescrutiny.

Reynolds News

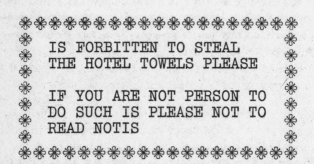

IS FORBITTEN TO STEAL
THE HOTEL TOWELS PLEASE

IF YOU ARE NOT PERSON TO
DO SUCH IS PLEASE NOT TO
READ NOTIS

Notice in Tokyo hotel

On board the train, trapped by falls of earth at Wilmington, were 1½ passengers, mostly female.

Express and Echo (Exeter)

So far, however, such worries seem premature. The cautious businessman of 1976 seems more inclined to sit on his hands and sprint to the finish line.

Purchasing World

When my husband reads in bed on warm nights he puts a collander over his head. He says it keeps off the flies, shades his eyes from the light and lets in air at the same time.

Letter in *Good Shopping* quoted in
New Statesman's 'This England' column

Miss O'Neill said Wardlow picked up an axe and struck her twice on the head with it. She was in bed at the time. Shortly afterwards, he hit her with a can of soup. 'He opened it then and we both had the soup,' she said.

Edinburgh Evening News

A CIRCUS MAN in Bor, Yugoslavia, who has already eaten more than 22,500 razor blades, a ton of brassware, cutlery, nuts, bolts and assorted ironware, has now bought himself a bus – which he intends to eat within the next two years.

Sunday Mirror

AIRLINE STOPS FOR A MOUSE

The pilot of a Britannia airliner brought his plane to a halt while taxiing for take-off yesterday to avoid hitting a mouse. The 112-seat plane, owned by the BKS airline, was setting out on a flight from Newcastle upon Tyne to London. Passengers were not told why the pilot stopped the airliner. A spokesman for BKS said later: 'He saw a mouse run across in front of the plane and pulled up to let it pass.'

He added: 'I have been in aviation for 22 years, but I have never heard of an action like this before.' The take-off was delayed only a few seconds and the incident was described in the plane's log as 'delayed due to conflicting traffic'.

Sun

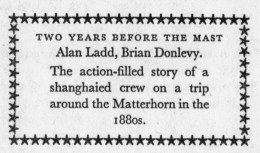 **Wheel changing.** The square wheel is located below the luggage compartment.

1970 Simca 1100 driver's handbook

> ★★★★★★★★★★★★★★★★★★★★★★
>
> TWO YEARS BEFORE THE MAST
> Alan Ladd, Brian Donlevy.
> The action-filled story of a shanghaied crew on a trip around the Matterhorn in the 1880s.
>
> ★★★★★★★★★★★★★★★★★★★★★★

Fort Lauderdale News

Parties up to 1,000 can and have been done.

Restaurant advertisement

PARKYNS – to the memory of Mr Parkyns, passed away September 10. Peace at last. From all the neighbours of Princes Avenue.

Leicester Mercury

You too can know the confidence and comfort of a firm denture if you sprinkle your plate every morning with Dr Thompson's Powder. You can laugh, talk and enjoy your meals all day long. Forget your false teeth, start using Dr Thompson's TODAY.

Advert in daily paper

Mrs D. G. Jarvis of Spencer Road has just returned from a visit in Ohio to see her mother. Knows the facts of life now.

Glen Ridge (New Jersey) paper

If he's stopped breathing, remove any obstruction such as false teeth or food, and immediately apply the 'kiss-of-life' (mouth-to-mouth breathing), the technique of which I'll describe next month.

Family Circle

Fruit vendor Tiago Machado, who was reported to have seen 'little green men' come out of a flying saucer when it landed near Sao Paulo, said yesterday that he had been misquoted. They were little red men, he declared.

Sussex paper

Edwards said he was sitting on the bench to rest his leg. He was frightened when he saw Skinner coming over and got out the knife to protect himself. The only reason he carried it was to chip splinters off his wooden leg. He also used it to help his girl friend cut up parsnips.

Eastern Daily Press

Only seven people attended the annual meeting of North Hanwell Residents' Association on Monday, out of a total membership of nearly 200. The meeting was held at St Christopher's Church Hall, Hanwell. The Secretary blamed the lack of attendance partly to the fact that the Church Hall's main door was locked.

Middlesex County Times

Three horses were found running loose in the parking lot of the Olin Ski Company, Smith Street, last night. Officer William Saraceno told them to leave, and they did, police say.

Middletown Press (Connecticut)

Not to be outdone by other artists, John Totten and his banjo along with several friends and their banjos will provide an instrumental interlude which itself should be worth the price of admission (which by the way is free).

                                        Massachusetts paper

I bought a few of your indigestion tablets last week. Now I feel a new man. (Original may be seen on request.)

                                        Advert in *Sheffield Star*

Without a word of warning the cows dashed out.

                                        Motor Cycling

A reception was held at the home of the groom and the happy couple left afterwards for their honeymoon at Coleshill near Birmingham. The bride travelled in her birthday outfit.

                                        Blaydon Courier

Dear Madam,
With reference to your blue raincoat, our manufacturers have given the garment in question a thorough testing, and find that it is absolutely waterproof. If you will wear it on a dry day, and then take it off and examine it you will see that our statement is correct.

                    Your obedient servant,
                        Blank & Co, Drapers

            FOUND, White fox-terrier dog.
            Apply with name on collar to
            51 Park Terrace, NW1

                                        Daily Telegraph

After eight years' searching the Parish Register for a name to match the initials H. W. P. on a stone slab in his church, the Rev. Phillip Randall, of Eye, near Peterborough, has solved the mystery. The initials stand for Hot Water Pipe.

Sunday Mirror

Onlookers who saw a car mount the pavement in Northwood Road and crash into the back of a van, could see no driver in the wandering car. But Mrs Pauline Harris of Jason Court, who admitted driving carelessly, told Croydon magistrates: 'I bent down to pick something off the floor of the car. My handbag, five library books and some flower pots had slid on to the floor.'

Croydon Advertiser

A woman thought it a strange request when a man who asked her if she wanted her drive re-surfaced, then persuaded her to rub his back with talcum powder, Warwick magistrates heard this morning.

Warwick Advertiser

Visitors to the well of Norwich Castle have been getting a wish on the cheap. Instead of dropping genuine coins down the 110 ft well in return for the traditional wish, some people have been tossing in make-believe money.

Eastern Daily Press

It is illegal for anyone to shoot or attempt to capture a wild horse from the cockpit of an aeroplane while flying over government territory.

US Air Travel

The service was conducted by the Rev. Charles Hensby MA, the bridegroom. The wedding was of a quiet nature owing to the recent death of the bride.

Blackpool Times

PUBLIC HEALTH PROBLEM

*

SPECIAL COMMITTEE TO SIT ON BED BUG

Liverpool paper

I would like your help concerning my receiver which has developed a fault. I find that when I turn up the contrast control to its proper setting, I get a dirty picture.

Practical Television

Recent tests conducted by a zoologist prove that grass-hoppers hear with their legs. In all cases the insects hopped when a tuning fork was sounded nearby. There was no reaction to this stimulus, however, when the insects' legs had been removed.

Corning Glass Works Magazine

After the boat had been secured above the wrecked galleon the apparatus was set in motion by the captain's 18-year-old daughter, Veronica. Within an hour she was yielding her treasure to the excited crew.

Florida paper

Until a few weeks ago Miss Fritz had planned to become a nun, but this week she decided to become a striptease artist instead.

Johannesburg Sunday Times

How about this for service? I took a wristwatch into a jeweller's here in town to be repaired. On Monday I collected it. Nothing unusual in that, you might say, until I tell you when I took it to be mended.

It was twenty-six years ago! I was not then 15 years old and I forgot to collect it. Months went by and I hadn't the nerve to go in and ask for it. I left it so long I thought they must have sold it. But on Monday I had cause to go into the shop again, so I asked, on the off-chance, whether it was still there.

Sure enough, the son of the previous owner of the shop found it for me. It still had on it the ticket in my maiden name which was put on it, by his father! The jeweller said his record for holding a watch before was eight years, so he suggested I write to you about it.

I wasn't charged a penny. I think the jeweller was so surprised that I had turned up after all those years.

Daily Mirror

One on the outside who criticizes the placement of square pegs in round holes should be sure that there are not more round holes and square pegs than there are square holes and round pegs. Even if this is not the case the critic should be certain that round holes are not a more serious problem than square ones, and he should withhold his criticism unless he is quite sure that it is better to leave round holes unfilled than it is to fill them partially with square pegs.

American Journal of Public Health

A minute later, Thomson fouled Jardine and the Rangers full back turned to retaliate. The players clashed, Jardine went down and Thomson was sent off protesting furiously. Fishing broke out on the terracing and many arrests were made.

Sunday Times

You will find that a draught excluder is effective for the base. You could make one yourself with a sand-filled 1234 Warm – Ad Feature Friday – Reverse indent right – fabric 'sausage'.

Lancashire Evening Post

He announced that the Commission proposed to give £30 million towards the provision of five goats for the protection of fishery up to the 200-mile limit.

Irish Times

Once he found a cat with a broken leg. He cut it off and strapped on a stamp. The cat lived 14 years.

Psychic News

She also said she had informed both hospitals that her husband was on the anti-clothing tablets.

Sheffield Star

Upton church's new organist is Mr Arthur G—. He is secretary of the local Outward Bound Association and is simple.

Worcester Journal

Whenever journalist John Montfort rings up his office, he does so literally. He has a voice in a million, which sets bells ringing along the line as soon as he speaks. The bells make it impossible for anyone on the private line at Southern Television's Dover newsroom to understand what Montfort is saying. That's not all. Sometimes the Dover office telephone bell actually starts ringing, too.

No one knew what the trouble was – until Mr Montfort, a sub-editor working at Southampton, complained to the Post Office. They analysed his voice and discovered it set up sound waves at exactly 500 cycles a second.

Last night a Post Office spokesman said: 'The frequency set up electric relays on the line and accounts for the ringing tone in the earpiece and the bell going off again.'

The chance of anyone having a voice pitched at exactly 500 cycles a second is about one in a million, said the spokesman. He added that an electrical adjustment had been made to the telephone bell at the Dover office. Now nobody is summoned by bells whenever Mr Montfort is on the line.

Sun

MAN SHOT DEAD BY HIS GUN DOG

Police last night named the killer of a man shot in the back. It was his gun dog, Sylvie. Police said Jean Marie Devaux, a 23-year-old hunter, placed his loaded rifle in the back seat of his car with Sylvie before going on an expedition near Le Havre, Northern France.

When he opened the door Sylvie sprang out, catching a paw in the trigger guard. The rifle went off, killing Devaux instantly. Tests on the rifle revealed Sylvie's paw print.

Daily Sketch

After tea, Mrs R— gave an amusing talk, with slides, on Baboo, her pet baboon. She said that although some people were scared by such a large animal, she felt completely at home with him, having spent over 15 years in Africa with her husband.

From a club newsletter

In the handicrafts exhibition at Wordsley Community Centre, the contribution of the Misses Smith was 'smocking and rugs' and not 'smoking drugs' as stated in last week's report.

The County Express (Stourbridge)

Keep butter and milk cool by standing under an inverted flower-pot in a draught in a basin of water to which half a cup of vinegar has been added.

Evening paper

His father spent a lifetime in the same occupation, so it might be said that Mr Longbottom was born, not with a silver spoon in his mouth, but with a cobbler's last.

Bradford Telegraph & Argus

Mr and Mrs Vera Boyd of Hart Road are the proud parents of a son born to Mr and Mrs Woodrow Boyd of Shereville.

Hammond (Indiana) Times

While a nurse was bathing off the coast of Scotland she was caught by the tide and, keeping her presence of mind, floated five miles to the Isle of Wight coast, where she swam ashore.

American paper

A MOTORIST, THE LAW, AND AN ASS

If you have a donkey beside you is it safe to drive? Magistrates at Totnes, South Devon, had to decide this yesterday when a man appeared charged with not having proper control over his small Citroen car.

Peter Cox, principal of Dartington College of Arts, Dartington, near Totnes, pleaded not guilty to the charge.

Constable Kenneth Arthur told the Court: 'As the vehicle drew near I saw the backside and tail of a donkey through the windscreen and very close to the driver. On causing the defendant to stop, I confirmed that the animal was a donkey.' PC Arthur said the rear seat of the car had been removed and Cox's wife was sitting in the back holding the halter of the donkey, which was in a standing position. The front passenger seat had been removed. The prosecution contended that Cox did not have proper control because his visibility was restricted.

Cox said the donkey was very tame. He produced a photograph showing that the driver could see between the top of the donkey and the roof of the car and to either side of the car. While he was being cross-examined the Bench stopped the proceedings and dismissed the case.

Guardian

Weidenfeld and Nicolson, who recently published *The Nightclerk*, by Stephen Schneck, would like to remind all booksellers that the book begins in the middle of a sentence on Page 9.

Bookseller

When his wife refused to cook him a meal, a man cut the plugs off every electrical appliance in the house. She retaliated by attacking him with a stair-rod while he was in the lavatory.

Surrey Herald

An interesting address on 'The National Care of the Child'
by Miss Palmer was much appreciated by all, and Mrs Lever
in a short address made an appeal for the use of the humane
killer.

Berkshire paper

Alderman Johnston moved that, pending the passing of the
street by-law, that all vehicles on Columbia Street be required to keep to the left going up and to the right going
down.

The British Columbian

It was announced at this time that the final practice for the
Children's Christmas programme will be hell on Saturday
afternoon between 2.00 and 3.00.

Ohio paper

Smooth and green and taut as a billiard-table I stepped on
to the Centre Court last week. A first and last appearance.

Sunday paper

Arrangements for teas at the Church Bazaar were in the
hands of Mrs C—, the daughter of the Archdeacon and a
lady member of the congregation.

Kent paper

All dogs found on the USG farm not accompanied by their
parents will be killed.

Kansas paper

Bus conductor KK 46793 had never stopped his No 19 double-decker so that a passenger could enjoy the view – until yesterday. And he had never been asked if he was an impostor – until yesterday.

But then he had never had a passenger riding-to-rule in protest against the busmen's work-to-rule. The protest began with a loud roar, as the green Hants & Dorset bus left Westover Road, Bournemouth. It was ex-Civil Servant Mr Kampara Ahmed announcing to the conductor that he intended to pay his fare – in accordance with Section 5 of the rule book.

Mr Ahmed, 75, bearded and clutching a walking stick, produced a £1 for his 2s 11d fare. First he wanted to know: 'Are you the conductor?' Uniformed conductor KK 46793 replied: 'No, I'm a lorry-driver.' 'Well then,' said Mr Ahmed, 'where is your authorization from the traffic commissioners?'

Eventually the ticket was given. Then came another pause. Under Section 6, the conductor must duly assure the passenger that the ticket is new. Then, under the statutory orders and regulations covering public service vehicles, Mr Ahmed asked for the bus to be stopped at a request stop. He did not want to get off. The rule book doesn't say he has to.

When the time came for Mr Ahmed to leave the bus, Section 4 of the rule book made his duty clear. He had to stay in his seat until the bus was stationary. This accomplished it was time for peace talks, the offer to shake hands. But it was refused. Said conductor KK 46793: 'I don't have to shake hands with you or give you my name. *It's not in the regulations.*'

Daily Mail

Ducking under crossing gates and running behind a west-
bound freight train, an electric passenger train which he
was trying to catch struck and mangled Henry Rasku of
122 Lockman Avenue today.

Evening Post (USA)

**The fire was discovered by Frances Boltz, 19, who
lives with her mother, Mrs Nellie Beltz, at the
2610 address. Jacob F. Blatz, father and husband,
is in the Georgetown Hospital recovering from
illness.**

Washington Post

In the final instalment of Anton Mikulencak's article in the
Granger News last week, the text as printed read: 'Nobody
did not see me drink here.'
    It should have read: 'Nobody did not seen me drink here.'
The *News* regrets this error and is glad to make this correc-
tion.

Granger (Texas) *News*

The Bishop of — who was enjoying the balmy morning
driving his car, after a laborious Sunday, gave the hounds a
'view halloa' when the second fox broke, and the gallant
Master rewarded his Lordship with the brush when hounds
bowled him over.

Provincial paper

A FOUR-LETTER word inspired a girl to strip naked yesterday. The girl, aged twenty-five, was fully clothed when she saw the word on a building sign . . . 'shed'.

So she did . . . and shed all her clothes. Then, without a stitch, she carried on walking along Euston Road, London. She was eventually driven off in a police car and later went to hospital. The girl told police that when she saw the sign she did 'what comes naturally'.

Daily Mirror

A wooden leg has been hung up in the bar of the Fox and Hounds at Singleton, in Sussex. It turned up in a local cowshed and someone remembered that the village carpenter had made it for a three-legged bull 40 years ago.

Sun

AN ENGLISH PUB IN NEW YORK'S GREENWICH
VILLAGE
an authentic pub serving genuine English scones
Village Voice quoted in the *Sun*

Sir, – I would not presume to object to the Road Research Board's playing statistical games with their fragments of information (your report on 27 July), but it would be well for them to realize that such a phrase as 'of the remaining 80 per cent, 24 per cent (28 drivers)' is less precise, scientific, and meaningful than '28 of the 141 drivers'.

It is probably only a matter of time before a mathematically minded bishop informs us that of the disciples chosen by Jesus no fewer than 8.3 per cent betrayed Him.

Yours faithfully, H. L. EVANS,
Lecturer in Religious Education, Bangor
The Times

Marinade the steak in the sauce for at least two hours, then cook a hot grill, basting with the sauce at frequent intervals. Alternatively, pour off sauce after marinading, heat separately, and let your guests pour it over themselves.

Recipe in Ohio newspaper

The first essential in the treatment of burns is that the patient should be removed from the fire.

First Aid Manual

There was a good number present at the S— Bible class on Monday and a keen discussion took place on the subject 'Are there stages in Sin?' On Monday night a practical class was held.

Welsh paper

Miss Mary Salter rendered three vocal solos and a return to orchestral music was greatly appreciated.

Surrey paper

The water-soaked contents, which had lain in the metal chest for 50 years, were patted dry with paper towels and spread on a table for examination. Among these was Mrs Helen Lancing, who played the piano for the monument dedication 50 years ago.

New York State paper

Some 200 years later, about 1858, the old school fell into disuse, but the old building was used for a time as a barn. A manager in one corner still survives.

Merseymart

A friend of mine expecting some visitors to tea at her country cottage one afternoon this week, popped some scones into the oven. An hour later she was about to step into the bath when horror-stricken she remembered them. Not even stopping to grab a towel, she dashed naked downstairs into the kitchen. Her hand was on the oven handle when she heard a knock on the back door. She was panic-stricken. For she was sure her caller was the baker who, if there was no reply, would open the door and leave the bread on the kitchen table.

She darted into the nearest haven: the broom cupboard. The back door clicked open. But then, appalled, my friend heard footsteps coming across the kitchen towards the broom cupboard. The door opened. And there stood an astonished gasman. He had come to read the meter – which is in the cupboard. My friend blushed deeply – and then explained: 'I'm so sorry – I was expecting the baker ...' The gasman said 'Oh!' Then he said 'Sorry, mum.' And tipping his cap politely he carefully closed the door again and walked out of the house.

Letter in *Sunday Express*

A baby sitter mixed up identical twins who had been kept in separate cots. Their parents, Captain and Mrs Douglas Wood, of Lubbock, Texas, have taken the twins back to hospital to have their footprints checked, so they can tell which is which.

Daily Express

People on a council caravan site at Bricket Wood, Herts, have been told by St Alban's Rural Council that they cannot keep cats or dogs, but a budgerigar, a parrot, or even an ostrich would be allowed. This was stated last night by the National Canine Defence League, who were arranging for a 6-ft ostrich to be delivered at the site.

Daily Telegraph

Ladies' hats never worn coat and jackets good quality fit
middle aged lady size 10–12 daughter in Australia going
cheap.

Herald (Luton)

Mrs Rose Brown, of London Road, East Grinstead, died on
Tuesday of last week at her home. She was 75, and had been
a resident for 60 years. Mrs Brown leaves a widower, Arthur
James, and a son, Michael, both senior partners of J. Rose &
Co, a removals contractor. Cremation was at Surrey and
Sussex Crematorium, on Monday, and from an early scrum
their fly-half kicked well into the corner for their winger to
score a try.

Sussex paper

**1975 Cortina 1600, white with black interior, taxed
MOT, £950, consider smaller older car, part exchange
for wife.**

Diss Express

Put the minced steam into a bowl, then turn steam out on to
a plate and make small indentation in the centre.

Irish Weekly Examiner

 CUSTOMERS SHOULD NOTE
THAT ANY COMPLAINTS
OF INCIVILITY ON THE
PART OF OUR STAFF WILL
BE SEVERELY DEALT WITH

Notice in shop

As to the matter of the table being smashed, it was not wilfully broken, but collapsed while two people were dancing on it.

Watford Echo

Mr Len Benson of 3 Bury Hill, Thornton-in-Cleveland, asks us to say he has no connection with a manure smell in the village.

Middlesbrough Evening Gazette

A Fenstanton meat dealer, accused of assault, alleged that a bucket of water was thrown over him by the manager of St Ives public abbatoir before he hit the manager in the face with a bullock's hoof, weighing 5 lbs.

Hunts Post

Zurich, 20 Aug. A Swiss couple who went on holiday to Hong Kong have returned without their poodle Rosa after a traumatic experience in a Chinese restaurant.

They told the newspaper *Blick* that they asked a waiter over to their table and pointed to the poodle while they made eating motions to show they wanted it to be fed.

Eventually the waiter appeared to understand and took Rosa off into the kitchen. About an hour later he came back with their main dish and when they picked up the silver lid they found their poodle roasted inside, garnished with pepper, sauce and bamboo shoots. The couple, suffering from emotional shock, decided to return to Zurich immediately.

The Times (by permission)

At an early age Jacob succeeded in saving enough money by his drawings to enable him to go to Paris to study. For two years he lived near Penury, in London.

South African paper

A printing error last week caused confusion, the price for this smartly modernized semi-detached horse in excellent position is £9,750.

Kidderminster Shuttle

. . . and remember you can make a wonderfully nourishing broth from the remains if you have an invalid in the house.

Notice in butcher's

Enormous crowds of day trippers came to South Shields and found unallowed happiness and recreation on the beach.

Shields Gazette and Shipping Telegraph

● When washing windows, add a small quantity of vinegar to the water. This will keep the flies away as well as cleaning them.   *Love Affair*

President Nixon's foreign policy adviser, Dr Henry Kissinger, has postponed a visit to Japan, due to tart this weekend.

Evening Gazette, Teesside

The three men were allegedly involved in a mock duel with home made words in front of the Liquor Store in Main Street.

Virgin Islands paper

Dennis Shamblin, 102, who recently applied for a marriage licence in Nitro, West Virginia, to marry Mamie Gibson, 60, says he does not plan to have children. 'My eyes are giving me trouble,' he explained.

Los Angeles Times

Not long after the Second World War a family called Wallishauser lived in Hechingen near Stuttgart. Like other German families during this period the Wallishausers lived in a chronic state of hunger. They waited for the food parcels sent to them by their American relatives with gratitude and impatience.

A new parcel arrived and Mrs Wallishauser saw that it contained a tin filled with fine grey powder which she assumed was instant soup. She told her family that supper this evening would be rather special, and, in a spirit of generosity, she invited an elderly cousin who lived near by to share the meal with them.

The soup powder proved to be rather insubstantial and Mrs Wallishauser added a little semolina to give it body. Everybody sat down, enjoyed their food; they declared the soup to be the best they had tasted in a long while; the elderly cousin had three helpings.

By the next post Mrs Wallishauser received a letter from her American relatives saying that they had included in their last food parcel a small tin filled with the ashes of their dead grandmother who had wished her remains to be interred in German soil.

Report in *France Soir* related in *True Stories*
by Christopher Logue

FOR SALE, a cross-cut saw by a Willard man with newly sharpened teeth.

Willard Company News

In a piano recital at the Richland School auditorium last week, presented by Mrs Eula Bedgood's pupils, four murders on the program were inadvertently omitted from the story published in last week's issue of the Journal.

Richland Journal, Georgia

Q. *I have a football helmet, in good condition, that dates drum with a screen on top. Everybody around me is doing it. I have a steel drum.*

A. No, it is illegal. Garbage and trash collection are available in your area.

Fort Myers News-Press, Florida

Councillor Eric Hendrie drew attention to an item in the report which he said gave him considerable concern. This was that pigs had been seen to panic and run down a slope into a scalding tank. What concerned him was that if this could happen to pigs it could happen to the attendants.

Scotsman

Farmworker's wife Mrs Josephine Chapman claimed that the estranged wife of her next-door neighbour did not wear knickers when she and her husband visited them.

So, it was alleged at the Old Bailey today, she set fire to their house.

Evening News

PREGNANT WOMAN BITES PC

Headline in *Epping and Ongar Gazette*

The librarian at the Building Research Station was somewhat puzzled by the demand for old copies of the *Daily Telegraph*. This too from the plumbing section, who seemed to be showing unexpected interest in right-wing politics. It emerged eventually that the standard test of a good flush is the ability to swallow half a *Daily Telegraph*.

New Scientist

HIS LORDSHIP: I suppose the word 'horse' in the rule does not include an aeroplane?

COUNSEL: No, I think not.

HIS LORDSHIP: It ought to, it is much the same thing.

COUNSEL: I think that it was put in for the relief of the archdeacon.

The Times Law Report

There she lives entirely surrounded by politics and animals
– MP father, mother a councillor, three horses, three Great
Danes all of whom sleep on her bed (there's also a brother
who has given up writing for *Tribune*).

Observer

Focus on Sweden
Mildred Carpen continues her journey through Portugal.

Providence Journal, Rhode Island

Blank's Restaurant where good food is an unexpected
pleasure.

Advert in *Richmond & Twickenham Times*

Neighbours who on seeing the blaze helped save the garage,
about 10 ft from the house, notified a white rabbit inside it.

Lewiston (Idaho) *Tribune*

Mr — was elected and has accepted the office of People's
Churchwarden. We could not get a better man!

Parish magazine

The writer, after making a purchase at the above-mentioned
factory, happened to sit down with his wife and three
children supplied by Walker Bros and greatly appreciated
by we Dublin people.

Letter to Dublin paper

TOILETS OUT OF ORDER
Use platforms 3-4, 7-8
Sign at New South Wales station

Sir, Recently we witnessed a 50p coin, tossed for the usual reason that one tosses a coin, land on its edge and remain so standing. We should like to record this realization of an event traditionally accorded a probability of zero.
We are, yours faithfully,
SUSAN M. CHAMBERS
PETER McLEOD
BRYAN J. T. MORGAN
MRC Applied Psychology Unit, 15 Chaucer Road, Cambridge

Letter in *The Times*

'I wish he wouldn't wear his old sports jacket – it makes him look a freak,' said Mrs Omi, wife of Brighton ex-officer showman who wears a 3-inch ivory ring in his nose, 5-inch daggers in his ears, and is dyed blue all over.

Daily Express quoted in *New Statesman*

A neurotic man who, during periodic fits of depression, takes his false teeth out and jumps on them, is to get half the cost of a new set from Dorset Health Committee 'on the grounds of hardship'.

News Chronicle quoted in *New Statesman*

Witness said that on Christmas Eve Mrs Smith left Mr Smith alone like a dog, with only his pyjamas.

News Chronicle

The other motorist involved declared that Mr H— smelled of drink. So did a policeman.

Daily Express

WANTED, Abingdon – Between £3,350 – £3,850, available for modern home with three bedrooms and garage or space for schoolmaster.

Advert in *Oxford Mail*

Two days later a woman walked into the Wigan Borough Police Station, thumped a large parcel on the information room desk and told them the contents were the old men mentioned in the *Evening Chronicle*.

Manchester Evening Chronicle

The lake at Danson Park has been remarkably immune from drowning accidents. There have been a number of fatalities but very few accidents.

Local paper

Miss Ruby Yates suddenly reveals a delicious sense of comedy, and is quite irresistible in black pyjamas, over her kidneys and bacon.

Provincial paper

Over the range from about 450 degrees centigrade to upwards of 500 degrees centigrade, the coal passes through a phase of elasticity during which it can be moulded between the fingers like putty.

Elements of Fuel Technology

It has long been a journalistic commonplace, a nutshell maxim in the Fleet Street novitiates that while 'Dog Bites Man' is not news 'Man Bites Dog' is news. . . . If 'Diner Bites Dinner' is not felt at the sub-editor's table to be superlatively newsworthy, 'Dinner Bites Diner' stands in an altogether different class. . . .

There are restaurants in France where you may select your lobster not yet put to the blush by any culinary contact or disguise. In such an establishment a customer complained that the crustacean paraded for his approval was not fresh. Whereupon, according to his evidence, the restaurant proprietor waved it under his nose shouting, 'Not fresh? Smell it!' This invitation he accepted but, so the restaurateur contended, went beyond its terms, peering at it in a manner calculated to cause it annoyance or irritation, so that the sequel was the natural and probable consequence of his own act.

That sequel was that the denizen of the deep, with well-judged precision, reached out a claw and seized the tip of the customer's nose, nor would it let go until it had drawn blood or (as one report suggests) actually removed the extremity of the (to it) intrusive organ, thereby causing the plaintiff pain and suffering and necessitating an operation by a distinguished plastic surgeon (or, as the French so delicately put it 'aesthetic surgeon'). The court found against the restaurateur and ordered him to pay the Franc equivalent of £100 damages and a £3 fine.

From *Straws in My Wig* by Richard Roe

A prime cause of the poultry industry's £5 million a year loss on cracked eggs was explained yesterday by Dr T. C. Carter, director of the Poultry Research Centre in Edinburgh: Some hens stand on tiptoe to lay – and consequently their eggs drop harder to the floor.

Daily Express

HARO

Mrs Thomas Jennings's classes for children of pre-kindergarten age will be resumed on Mondays, Wednesdays and Fridays, from 9 to 12 o'clock. A slight smack will be served about 10.30.

Connecticut paper

It appears to us that Mr Dewey would have been wielding a double-edged sword in the shape of a boomerang that would have come home to plague him and beat him by a large majority.

Northampton (Mass.) *Hampshire Gazette*

Sipping hot tea, as many players do, Andrews served, drove and volleyed with brilliant energy and control.

Sussex paper

The cook at a Swiss hotel lost a finger in a meat-cutting machine and put in a claim to his insurance company. The company suspected negligence and sent a representative for an on-the-spot investigation. He asked to be allowed to work the machine – and lost a finger. The cook got his insurance money.

Weekend

Four policemen surrounded 26-year-old chef Alan Williams when he got off a train at Shoreham, Sussex, yesterday. A report telephoned down the line had said that a man carrying a gun in a shoulder-holster was on the train. 'Hand it over,' said one of the policemen, pointing to the bulge in Mr Williams' jacket.

Mr Williams fumbled inside his jacket and produced – a fish. 'I bought it for my cat,' he explained. 'I was in a hurry and stuffed it inside my jacket.'

Mr Williams of Woodview, Shoreham, said last night: 'It was a frightening experience – quite a crowd gathered. I realize the police were only doing their duty.'

Sun

'*Dear Milkman: Starting today leave one Jersey on Mondays and Thursdays but none on Saturday – then leave 1 thick cream on Tuesdays and 1 yoghourt on Wednesdays with 1 quart of Jersey. Then leave 1 quart of Jersey on Friday with thick cream, for the weekends leave 2 Jerseys and 1 yoghourt on a Saturday and 1 thick cream on a Sunday. Please alternate this for me. If the thick cream falls on a Saturday leave 1 Jersey with it then. Empty bottles are in the garage. Climb through the side window. Garage is locked.*'

Shirley Glick in *Reader's Digest*

When the baby is done drinking it must be unscrewed and laid in a cool place under a tap. If the baby does not thrive on fresh milk it should be boiled.

Women's magazine

The concert held in the Good Templars' Hall was a great success. Special thanks are due to the Vicar's daughter who laboured the whole evening at the piano, which as usual fell upon her.

South African paper

Before Miss Jenkinson concluded the concert by singing 'I'll walk beside you' she was prevented with a bouquet of red roses.

Sussex paper

HARO

Middlesex County Council is to be represented in Twickenham Fair procession by West Middlesex main drainage
department. It is exhibiting a tableau of three decorated
vehicles depicting the stages through which sewage passes.

Surrey Comet

Said Mr Justice Vaisey: 'It is a fearful thing to contemplate
that, when you are driving along the road, a heavy horse
may at any moment drop from the sky on top of you.'

Daily Graphic

The coroner (Mr W. Bentley Purchase) recorded an open
verdict. He said: 'In many years of experience I have made
the observation that if a woman is going to commit suicide
she rarely takes her handbag.'

Evening Standard

I wish to take up lessons on the saxophone, but have high
blood pressure, heart murmur, and punctured diaphragm.
Do you think it would be advisable?

Health column in *The Graphic*

Old-established manufacturer of suspension bridges requires door-to-door salesman.

African paper

(Here and in the item below we see Gobfrey Shrdlu at his
best. He is perhaps trying to tell us that the life we lead
is too humdrum. We should have imagination . . .)

FOR SALE – Cottage piano
made in Berlin, owner
getting grand.

Advert in The Pioneer

Slough Borough babies have their big chance at the baby
show. Entries can be made on the ground and during the
evening the last eight will contest the Berks and Bucks darts
championship.

Windsor, Slough & Eton Express

THE PEACOCK HOTEL
Every Wed and Sat
Come dancing to the Peacock Trio (all aged)
Bradford Telegraph and Argus

The set was carefully built and the variety of gropings on
stage provided constant interest.

Aberdeen Press and Journal

10.10 The story of one of the most public and astounding
medical successes this century – the discovery of a vaccine
to combat police.

Evening Times (Glasgow)

During the past few days three bicycles have been stolen
from Exeter streets. The police consider that a bicycle thief
is at work.

Western Morning News

Man doing heavy work requires old sports jackets, 38 in., cheap, also dozen babies napkins, 24 in., good condition.

Exchange & Mart

When the porter came out, they started throwing objects at him which he thought were bags of chicken noodle soup, but which the two defendants claimed were mud.

Beds and Bucks Observer

'Jesus forgives you,' born-again Charles Colson told James Weigall, after James pushed a chocolate pie in his face. 'Jesus told me to hit you with a pie because you are a fraud,' said James.

Chicago Daily News

The Rosyth-based fishery protection vessel HMS *Jersey*, investigating a report of a body in the English Channel, has recovered an inflatable woman three miles east of North Goodwin lightship.

Edinburgh Evening News

Sex and violence came into Jane Martin's life gradually. Then she became a Christian and matters escalated.

Essex County Standard

The meeting, at which Lady Carrington presided, was told by Mr Corning that they were anxious that parents should be encouraged to seek help from NSPCC inspectors or social workers before they injured their children.

Bucks Herald

HARO

The lad was described as lazy, and when his mother asked him to go to work he threatened to smash her brains out. The case was adjourned for three weeks to give the lad another chance.

Guardian

Miss Craig has been appointed to act as general supervisor of Work Area Six and not (as stated in our August issue) of Work Area Sex.

From a staff magazine

Mr J—, the Highways Committee chairman said: We intend to take the road through the cemetery – provided we can get permission from the various bodies concerned.

West London Observer

LEAVE REGULATIONS – *Section 3. When an employee absent from duty on account of illness dies without making application for advanced sick leave, the fact of death is sufficient to show a 'serious disability' and to dispense with the requirement of a formal application and a medical certificate.*

US Government order

We forwarded your enquiry re nettle tea to the writer of the recipe in our issue of 20 July, but have received a notification from his executors' solicitors to say that he is now deceased.

Gardening paper

For 30 years the two old friends met for supper every night. And for 30 years John Quartero, now passed 70, bottled up his anger. The trouble: his friend Joe Cocito made the ravioli sauce too hot – and as the years slipped by old Joe made it hotter and hotter.

Last night Quartero could take no more. Without a word he stood up and left. This morning they met in the street and chef Joe asked John why he had walked out. John's reply was dramatic. He whipped out a gun and shot his friend in the leg.

Accused of assault with a deadly weapon, old John tearfully told Miami police: 'I couldn't stand Joe's hot sauce any longer.'

Daily Express

A man, operated on at a Darlington hospital, had in his stomach: hay, bits of metal and porcelain, a razor blade, a file, stones, a pin, 4½d, a football coupon, matches, a hairgrip, a key, nails, a pair of dividers, a pen-nib, a knife, and a double-six domino. He recovered.

Daily Express

We make a speciality of gorillas and chimpanzees. They are wonderfully intelligent and can be trained right up to the human standard in all except speech. One of our directors, Mr Alec Jackson and his wife are both able to be tamed to live in captivity.

Irish paper

A competition was held for the oddest object found on the beach and the result was – 1, Mrs Thompson, 2, Mrs Robins, 3, Mrs Jackson.

Women's Institute bulletin

Needing evidence for an armed robbery, police obtained entrance to a house in Station Road and went from room to room searching for gnus.

Daily Telegraph

He was involved in the Normandy landings and first met his future wife at Rye, lust before D-Day.

The Keighley News

The local ladies, who were on duty in the church and elsewhere, were by no means ornamental additions to the gathering.

Hertfordshire paper

A great amount of useful information was given by the demonstrator. The height of her talk was how to bottle fruit without fruit, which needless to say attracted much attention.

Parish magazine

'The boy would be expected to foresee,' Judge Forbes added, 'that there is one thing a man does not want after having his Sunday dinner; that is to have his feet tickled.'

News of the World

A Hampshire friend reports that an entry in her eight-year-old son's diary has convinced her that strict discipline continues to be maintained in British boarding-schools. The entry reads: 'I must not clean my teeth with salad cream during prayers.'

Evening Standard

Mrs Raymond Hacken and Miss Evelyn Fothergill gave a surprise pink and white shower for Mrs Mahlon Owens on the Eaton lawn, attended by 33 people. One feature of the programme was a Caesarian operation which proved amusing.

Vermont paper

Asked if he had any of the stolen articles, the accused, James Smithers, replied: 'Yes, I have some of them at home and if you come and go with me now, I will give you them.'

Constable Weston said that at his home at Gilkes Land, Hindesbury Road, Smithers gave him a multi-coloured bath robe, seven shirts, three pairs of pants, two pairs of socks, one pouch of Ivorol, one shaving set, one pair of earrings, one window blind, one United States 5-cent piece, one torch light, and said 'These are all the things I got from Mrs Cox.'

The offence was alleged to be committed in January this year. Mrs Cox said she discovered certain articles missing when she was looking for the eighth, ninth and tenth books of Moses.

Barbados Advocate

Baby meals would cost 11p or 12p or four and half times more. British babies like children casserole best.

The Times

Mr Campbell, who was on the boat deck, jumped to the rails and threw a lifeboat to the drowning man.

Scots paper

£1,000 at death if within five years, with the option of continuing thereafter.

Insurance Company's leaflet

FLIES COMING INTO CONTACT
WITH THIS PREPARATION OF DDT
DIE WITHOUT HOPE OF RECOVERY

Label on bottle

Let us nip this political monkey business in the bud before it sticks to us like a leech.

Letter in *San Francisco Chronicle*

Inspector Jones said that the usual red herring of Mr Skinner's had been exploded – that there was a flat tyre.

Isle of Man paper

One of the many engagements that are always announced at the close of the season is that of Miss Caroline Stackley.

The World

Before going to sleep at night I read in bed for twenty
minutes. During that time I warm my feet by breathing *in*
through my nose and *out* through a length of rubber tubing
reaching from my mouth to my feet. Within five minutes I
am glowing with heat.

> Letter in *Daily Mail* quoted in *New Statesman*'s
> 'This England' column

A 30-year-old housewife – accused of stealing two tins of
meat from a supermarket – told Leamington magistrates
that she had 'never been the same' since she saw a man
running about in the nude. 'I have been under sedatives
from my doctor ever since,' she said.

> *Leamington Morning News*

Tight-rope walkers Roger and Betty Decugis, who wanted
their five-month-old daughter Christine christened on a
high wire slung 400 ft over Somerset's Cheddar Gorge, have
had their idea turned down by the Bishop of Clifton, the Rt
Rev. Joseph Rudderham. Now their daughter will be
christened in church – and then will be taken across the
wire on a motorcycle.

> *Daily Express*

Miss Smith told the *Evening Standard* today: 'He hit me on
the temple with his fist, and I was knocked into the ditch.
While I was lying there dazed something made me say to
him: "Thanks very much!" He replied in quite a refined
accent: "Oh, don't mention it." '

> *Evening Standard*

Mr Parker is also being married soon, but his ambitions lie elsewhere.

                                                        Yorkshire paper

John F—, the celebrated singer, was in a motor-car accident last week. We are happy to state he was able to appear the following evening in four pieces.

                                                        Bradford paper

Whenever eggs are cheap the fowls yield a fair supply, and when they become dear production stops.

                                                        Pall Mall Gazette

                    TO THE FAIRY GLEN
                     Five minutes walk
                  BEWARE HEAVY LORRIES
                                        Notice in North Wales

What is more beautiful for a blonde to wear for formal dances than white tulle? My answer – and I'm sure you will agree with me – is 'Nothing'.

                                Worcester (Mass.) Evening Gazette

It has usually been the custom to get some prominent gentleman to take the chair, but on this occasion the selection fell on Councillor Eastland.

                                                        Bristol paper

He believed that with the assistance of the ladies it would be possible to form a non-profit-making concern.

                                                        Church magazine

A letter addressed to 'Degenerate Bawd' in London has been correctly deciphered by the Post Office as being intended for the Central Electricity Generating Board, according to the February issue of *Power News*.

Evening Standard

CURRY EATING SPECIALIST IS FINED £5

A stranger in an Indian restaurant in Southend tried to demonstrate to Mr Arthur Flint how he should eat his curried chicken and rice. Mr Flint demonstrated his displeasure by pushing the curry in his face. In return, Mr Flint received a blow on the head with a chair.

At Southend court today the stranger, William Parkins, aged 28, a paint colour matcher, of Boston Avenue, Southend, pleaded guilty to assaulting Mr Flint and was fined £5 with £3 3s costs. Mr R. A. Shorter, prosecuting, said Mr Flint and a friend had ordered a meal when Parkins, sitting at a nearby table, spoke to them. He sat down uninvited and advised Mr Flint to drink a glass of water before eating the curry. Then he said he would show him how to prepare the meal, picked up the rice and poured it on the curry, and mixed it together. Mr Flint sat watching and then asked: 'Have you finished?' Mr Parkins said he had, whereupon Mr Flint picked up the plate and pushed it into his face.

The curry and rice ran down Parkins's clothing and following an argument, he left. Later, as Mr Flint sat eating a replaced meal, he felt a severe blow on the head and shoulders and on grappling with his assailant, found he had caught hold of the curry-stained Parkins. Police were called and Parkins told them: 'I hit him with a chair. My pride couldn't take it. He pushed me too far.'

In a statement he explained that he was only showing Mr Flint how to prepare his meal and added: 'He picked up the plate and pushed the whole lot in my face. I was shocked beyond belief because he seemed so friendly.'

Evening Standard

FOLIES PARISIENNE

SEE! NUDES IN THE WATERFALL
DARING FAN DANCE. VIRGIN AND THE DEVIL

Sensational dance of the Strip Apache
Les Beaux Mannequins de Parisienne
Continental and Oriental Nudes
Old Age Pensioners Monday

Advert in Leicester paper

'This budget leakage is something that's got to stop,' said the President, with what seemed to be more than a trace of irrigation in his voice.

Jackson (Missouri) State Times

. . . and a few moments after the Countess had broken the traditional bottle of champagne on the bows of the noble ship, she slid slowly and gracefully down the slipway, entering the water with scarcely a splash.

Essex paper

Three times Mr Robert L— tried to get back the 222-year-old violin which he claimed he lent to an aspiring 20-year-old girl musician in 1942. The musician, Miss F— claimed that the instrument was an outright gift with no strings attached.

Evening Standard

The customs search was continued when the ship arrived at Tilbury – and the half-ounce was found by a specially trained dog hidden in a hose reel.

Oldham Evening Chronicle

PARIS, 2 October – *An unknown woman who fell from a tower of Notre Dame cathedral today landed on an American, Veronica McConnell, aged 22, of Philadelphia. Both were killed. Miss McConnell arrived here last night in a tour party of 40.*

Reuter

The wife of a steelworker in Romford, Essex, complained that her husband's whiskers tickled her in bed. He was so attached to his beard, however, that he shaved off only one side, so that the cheek nearest to his wife should be smooth.

News agency story

A few years ago a Hungarian was travelling by train to Budapest. He had some bees in milk bottles with brown paper covering. Somehow the bees pierced the paper and climbed up the man's legs. To avoid being stung he explained his plight to women in the compartment, who withdrew.

He took off his trousers – and an express travelling in the opposite direction set up such a draught the trousers were whisked into the corridor. They wrapped round the neck of a ticket inspector, who was attacked by the bees. Someone pulled the communication cord, the train pulled up – and caught fire.

Officials noticed a man without trousers, and thought he was an escaped lunatic. He was arrested and strait-jacketed. It took the bee expert three days to convince asylum doctors that he was sane.

News agency story

Mrs Elaine Fox was told to order 250 brass taps for an Australian Government department. She misheard and must now explain delivery of a box of bra straps.

Tit-Bits

**Bathers are reminded that they must be fully
dressed upon entry into swimming pools and
must be fully dressed upon leaving swimming pools.**

Fort Belvoir Daily Bulletin

Would any friendly older couple with hours to spare like to
help bury family in house and garden.

Avon Advertiser

The future of financially troubled Randolph Manufacturing
Co may be decided this week, Sidney Crane, chairman of
Randy Industries Inc., told the Globe.

Randolph Manufacturing is a wholly owned subsidiary of
Randy and it has been ailing for some time. Canufacturing
said the Rananufacturing canvas footwanufacturing manu-
facturinanufacturing operationanufacturing has been
neanufacturing shutdown on on two or three occasions
incent once this week.

Boston Globe

Shrews burn up energy so fast that this search for food
occupies all their waking hours. Through the seasons,
through the raising of her young, through numerous
escapes from her enemies and forays for food, Miss Fisher
follows the fortunes of this tiny animal.

Review in *Washington Post*

Dear Sir, With reference to our letter re Majorca tour, the
flight you mention is completely booked, but we will
inform you immediately someone falls out, as usually
happens.

Letter from travel agent

Mr Robin Page, who has threatened to start an art form that involves stamping frogs to death, gave a demonstration of his ideas yesterday. Wearing a silver PVC suit, silver-painted helmet, and rubber knee-boots, he bored and pick-axed through the concrete floor of Better Books, in Charing Cross Road. Chips of concrete flew at the audience. After half an hour Page struck water. Mr Robert Cobbing, the manager, then said: 'This must stop.' Page, a leading member of the Destruction in Art Symposium, downed his shovel, sat in the hole, and drank a bottle of beer.

He said: 'I feel very good. I have no more doubts about anything. It is a beautiful hole. If somebody wants to buy it the price would be £125. It's a major work, but I'm open to offers.' Two girls in mini-skirts then paraded with placards protesting against the possible killing of chickens. Page was unrepentant. He said he would put frogs on a board on which questions were written about Destruction in Art. If the frogs gave the wrong answers they would be stamped to death.

Daily Express

A man I know locks up his alarm clock in a tin medicine chest (for extra noise) every night before retiring. To reach the key to open the chest to turn off the alarm he has to plunge his arm into a deep jug full of icy water where he dropped the key the night before. This is the only way he knows to be certain of waking up.

Sunday Graphic

As a Nottinghamshire licensee was driving his car along the A606 from Hickling Pastures, Nottinghamshire, a goat jumped on the seat beside him and he went the wrong way round a traffic island, Bingham magistrates were told yesterday.

Notts Evening Post

41 per cent of women who have never been married were
first married before their 20th birthday, the Census Bureau
reports.

Greenwich Time (Connecticut)

Sergeant Gibson was hit on the head, Constable Hope on
the arm, Constable Campbell, in the back seat, escaped
injury.

Daily Express

Staff should empty the tea-pot and
then stand upside down on the tea
tray.

Office notice

When Miss Dixie Janice Byram, daughter of Mr
and Mrs R. C. Byram of this city, became the bride
of Edward Hersey on Friday afternoon at 2 o'clock
at many friends here occurred last overshirt of lace.
Her hat was the First Presbyterian Church.

Winter Haven (Florida) *Herald*

God is Always At Hand To Help
in Adversity. Please write Box 3092.

Border Counties Advertiser

John Cardew stated that he had seen a large number of skulls
thrown up during an interment. He did not think that was a
proper thing. He would cry his eyes out if he saw it done to
his own.

Irish Times

The National Research Council of Canada has developed a pneumatic cannon that fires dead chickens at speeds of up to 620 mph.

Chemical and Engineering News

SUVA CITY COUNCIL – CHILDREN'S LIBRARY
Notice is hereby given that the Children's Library will be closed on Wednesday on the occasion of its official opening.

Fiji Times

BELFORT, France. A railman entered hospital at Belfort, France, for removal of his haemorrhoids and got his nose straightened. Dr Jean Barron told a Court who fined him £150 for the error: 'It struck me that the middle of his nose was bent.'

Southern Evening Echo

We apologize profusely to all our patrons who received, through an unfortunate computer error, the chest measurements of members of the Female Wrestlers Association instead of the figures on the sales of soybeans to foreign countries.

Saturday Review

Marie Theresa Robbins (21) unemployed, of no fixed abode, took exception when refused entry to the dance at Gremista. She had been told that she was improperly dressed – she was wearing a boiler suit and rubber boots. When she appeared in the Sheriff Court she admitted a breach of the peace at the dance hall, assaulting a doorman by pushing a fish supper into his face.

Shetland Times

Heavy rains again fell in Khartoum and vicinity last
Saturday night and several lakes have been formed
in various parts of the town, some of which are still
navigable. Mosquitos are not allowed to breed in
them, under penalty of a heavy fine.

Egyptian Mail

Strawberries, which by now should be well in season, are
unripened on the damp ground. Already many growers are
getting covered with a grey mould.

Manchester Evening Post

Lady with one child 2½ years old seeks situation as house-
keeper. oGod cook.

Advert in S. African Paper

. . . the bride wore a Spanish influenced dress with high
neck, and frills on the sleeves . . . The dress which was
gathered at the back fell gently to the floor.

Middlesex Advertiser and Gazette

AUDIENCE TRIED TO SPOIL PLAY BUT ST CHAD'S PLAYERS SUCCEEDED

Sutherland Echo

FOR SALE, Doctor's sailing dinghy and accessories. Doctor
no further use.

Advert in *Yorkshire Post*

On Tuesday for one day only there is a special presentation of the film of Jane Austen's *Pride and Prejudice*. The story weaves its way through murder, anonymous phone calls, obscene letters and drug addiction to a deserted showroom in New York's rag trade district where the final drama is played out.

Enfield Gazette

Sir – Mr Victor Constad's letter of 30 September is of particular interest to me, in view of a personal experience some years before the war. I had parked my sports car in Croydon, and on emerging from a shop where I had been making a certain purchase I found a crowd surrounding the vehicle. Apparently a small boy on a bicycle, pedalling head down over the handlebars, had ridden straight into the radiator. His injuries were luckily only superficial but certainly spectacular.

The point of interest is that, on the arrival of a policeman, two members of the crowd were prepared to swear that I had actually hit the boy while driving. Fortunately for me the shopkeeper and a number of other witnesses were able to establish the true circumstances. I do however feel that this bears out your correspondent's point.

Yours sincerely, W. D. PHILLIPS, Cheltenham
The Times

Sir, – The warning to all motorists – around the corner you are going to meet another damn fool – is particularly true to my uncle, who took a corner at fifty miles an hour on the wrong side of the road and was passed by another car doing exactly the same thing in the other direction. Without speaking a word the men got out of their cars, shook hands, and drove away.

John Rae, Hallam St, W1
The Times

After all, we are largely as nature made us, and Governor Smith's smile was born with him, just as were his liking for children and his derby hat.

Omaha Evening World-Herald

Evidence was given by PC Hart who described how he saw wrapping and later roll it into Smith eating from a paper a ball and throw it into the street.

Gloucester Citizen

Mrs Elizabeth Smith (Chairman) gave a talk on Spain, including a description of a bullfight at the luncheon meeting of Cowplain and Waterlooville Ladies Club.

Portsmouth and Southsea Evening News

La orquesta ejecutó el 'Good sabe the Queen', coreado por la concurrencia, lo mismó que el 'Forisa folley good fillow'.

La Nacion, Buenos Aires

A 17-year-old boy died in the New Plymouth hospital as a result of injuries received in a car crash at Inglewood. He was Rex Manton, who died less than two hours after the accident. His condition was reported tonight to be satisfactory.

Hamilton Times, New Zealand

Tradition says that the aborigines of the Patagonian region bathed their infants in icy water to toughen them. The aborigines are now extinct.

Philadelphia Enquirer

GEORGE ANTHONY MARTIN, of Salisbury, Rhodesia, who owed a firm £9 3s 4d, answered the firm's advertisement which offered £3 3s reward for his address. Martin won case in the magistrate's court and the reward was deducted from his debt.

Daily Express

I am an Indian, aged 19, and I'm in love with a 15-year-old Eurasian schoolgirl. I fell in love with her when she was 13, but I was forced to 'break off' with her recently. The reasons for this are (1) She does not seem to care for me of late; (2) She has started to mix up with a set of bad girls; (3) She thinks she can boss everybody. Also I have a suspicion that she thinks I love someone else. Have I done right by breaking away from her? What shall I do?

UNCLE JOE'S REPLY: I am getting rather 'fed up' with people who keep on writing on both sides of the paper, as you have done. The next time anybody does this, I'm going to throw his letter into the waste-paper basket and say nothing.

Singapore Free Press

WANTED, BEARDED MAN age 25–35. Must be (1) willing to shave and re-grow beard frequently, (2) available in London, and (3) have brown or dark hair. Substantial remuneration for successful candidate. Send letter and photograph (snapshot size, returnable) to Box Z 1634.

The Times

FIRE-EATERS, SWORD-SWALLOWERS, preferably with ecclesiastical experience required, May–June, Phone: WELbeck 2331.

The Times

Mr Jager, driving against Mr Pollock from the first tee, pulled his ball into the press tent and ran under the flooring.

Dundee Courier

LONELY LADY, 43, with little dog, seeks post.

Advert in *Exeter Express and Echo*

It is not considered polite to tear bits off your beard and put them in your soup.

Etiquette book

After Governor Baldridge watched the lion perform, he was taken to Main Street and fed twenty-five pounds of raw meat in front of the Fox Theatre.

Idaho Statesman

'Good,' muttered Armand Roche to himself, hiding a smile beneath the false black beard which he always carried in his portmanteau in case of an emergency.

Short story

Ted could not raise the cash necessary to purchase a house, and eventually in desperation he had to burrow.

Woman's Magazine

TREATED LIKE DOG BY WIFE
Husband cooked for 30 years

Daily Telegraph

NOTICE TO ALL EMPLOYEES
Some time between starting and quitting time, without infringing on lunch periods, coffee breaks, rest periods, storytelling, ticket-selling, holiday planning, and the rehashing of yesterday's TV programmes, we ask that each employee try to find some time for a work break.

This may seem radical, but it might aid steady employment, assure regular pay checks – Spielman Chevrolet Company of New York.

Daily Express

Sir, – Miss H. B. Pang's fervent affirmations in defence of monocles for women (16 September) reminds me of a dear lady friend of mine, who did her shopping carrying an eight-day timepiece with an engine whistle firmly attached to it.

When a reporter from a local newspaper asked her why she carried these accessories, she replied that they were very useful. At any time, she explained, someone might stop her in the street and ask her if she possessed an eight-day timepiece with a whistle attached – and she could always say 'Yes'.

B. PAXTON, Clayton, Manchester
Letter in *Picture Post*

Decrepit (officially, having reached the advanced age of 60) schoolmaster, speaking four languages fluently, late Cambridge scholar, late Indian Civil Service, seeks post carrying salary approximating to, say, half the wages received by miner or docker. (Decrepit golf handicap 5.) Write Box B 1989.

The Times

Miss Crichton pluckily extinguished the blaze while Herr Eckold pulled the orchestra through a difficult passage.

Daily Express

Advert in New Mexico paper

The helicopter abandoned its passive role and flew several low lasses over the strikers.

Daily Telegraph

The weather bureau had predicted up to six inches of snow in the metropolitan area; it had already deposited snow in parts of the Southeast.

New York Times

'The vast majority of those in the sports world are honest men,' Brickley said. 'The fact that a relative few have had contacts with the alleged betting ring could be serious or something relatively innocent. Maybe stupid, but relatively innocent.'

Another man who was arrested said 'On the far side of the moon the crust was thick and solid and meteorites merely blasted craters.'

Oakland Tribune (California)

WEIRD COLLECTION OF HARDWARE FOUND
IN MAN'S STOMACH

TOBATA, Japan. (AP) – Passers-by found 52-year-old Goichi Kawakami lying in the street, doubled up with pain. At Kyoritsu hospital doctors decided his stomach was inflamed. They operated.

Inside they found: 1 piece of wire, 13 razor blades, 1 fountain-pen, 1 toothbrush, 1 pencil, 1 pair of chopsticks, 1 bone from an umbrella, 21 nails and 41 other items of hardware – all, it appeared, swallowed during the last six months.

Kawakami explained: 'I was told at a festival they would give me a big prize if I ate hardware.'

Mississippi paper

PAYMASTERS NEVER FORGET

These letters, I am assured, have passed between Capt. X and the Army Paymaster.

Letter from Capt. X to Army Paymaster: 'I observe that my promotion to the rank of Captain is shown in orders as taking effect from 19 May 944. I therefore request that my account may be credited with £63,875 as representing arrears of pay now due.'

Letter from Army Paymaster to Capt. X: 'In reply to your letter, it is pointed out that since the date therein mentioned the Battle of Hastings has been fought, in the course of which a considerable deficiency of bows and arrows was brought to light.

'Since you appear to be the sole survivor of this incident, your liability in respect of this deficiency, the replacement value of which is estimated at £63,875 6s 8d, cannot be questioned. If therefore you will remit the sum of 6s 8d the matter can be dealt with *per contra* and may be considered closed.'

Peterborough in *Daily Telegraph*

There are some engineers who do not hesitate to associate
themselves in print with the forthright denunciation that
the project is a white elephant doomed to crash ere it is
feathered for full flight.

Technical paper

● Because elderly people find it difficult to climb the hill at
Castle Green, Kenilworth, a seat is to be provided at the top
by the District Council.

Leamington News

PARISIAN BEHEADED
FOR KILLING WIFE
BEFORE MISTRESS

St Louis Post-Dispatch

The two buses a day are to be withdrawn. Mr John Walker
said he could confirm that only 1.8 people were using the
bus on Saturdays; he had seen them.

North Somerset Mercury

Whilst snow is unprecedented at this time of year, especially
in the south of Ireland, it is certainly not unusual.

Cork Evening Echo

Both the long jump and the high jump were won by Victor
Ludorum.

Bedford paper

Sir, – People with a sense of humour do not write to a newspaper to argue about a sense of humour, except those people with a sense of humour who only write to a newspaper to point out that people with a sense of humour do not write to a newspaper to argue about a sense of humour.

Yours faithfully, HOWARD WYGE, SW10

The Times

Einstein theory led to arson

Because he disagreed with Einstein's theory of relativity Michael Victor Dobson, aged 27, went to Harrow School and set fire to and destroyed a shed, the prosecution said at Middlesex Area Sessions yesterday. Damage was estimated at £796. Mr Dobson, unemployed, of Aberdeen Road, Wealdstone, Middlesex, pleaded guilty to a charge of arson.

The Times

Case of double glazing

A policeman said yesterday about a man accused of being drunk, 'He was unsteady on his feet, his breath smelt of alcohol and his eyes were glazed.' Hugh Jones, aged 40, a postal executive, removed his right eye and said: 'It was bound to be glazed.'

'The other one was glazed too,' Police Constable John Harris retorted. Mr Jones, who was conditionally discharged for three months at Thames Court for being drunk, replaced his eye before leaving court.

The Times

Added Mrs Spragston, 'When Mrs Johns told me she had been intimate with my husband I refused to give her tea.'

Daily Express

THOSE TO REQUIRE BATHING PLEASE TO NOTICE THE CHAMBERMAID

Notice in Spanish hotel

Mrs Robert M. Hitch, President of the Poetry Society, is expecting an unusually large attendance. There will be no original poems read at the meeting tonight by members.

Savannah Evening Press (Georgia)

The scheduled concert at the Boston Museum of Fine Arts this afternoon has been cancelled. It was to have featured Viola da Gamba and her harpsichord.

Boston Post

We have printed, verbatim, all that Phillimore gives on the subject. Nor has Phillimore rested his facts on Prideaux alone. He quotes Ibid as his authority for paragraphs 3 and 4, both of which paragraphs confirm paragraph 2 based on Prideaux.

Nottingham Daily Express

Mrs Robert Lee Brown of Ithaca was organist, playing 'Clair de Lune', 'At Dawning', 'To a Wild Rose', and 'On Don Tino'.

Gratiot County Herald (Michigan)

Marble top dresser, walnut hall tree, bevel mirror, and J. A. Cobean 3-piece living-room suite.

Advert in *Shreveport Times* (Louisiana)

Miklos Levay, soaked to the skin, thumbed a lift from a lorry on the road between Balmazujvaros and Budapest in Hungary. In the back was an empty coffin. Levay climbed in and closed the lid.

Further down the road the lorry stopped again and another hitch-hiker climbed aboard. Later, when the rain stopped, Levay felt hot and stuffy inside the coffin. So he raised the lid and shouted, 'What's the weather like?'

His fellow hitch-hiker screamed with fear, jumped off the fast-moving truck in panic, broke a leg and suffered various other injuries. Later he took Levay and the driver, Janos Mihaly, to court, charging them with grievous bodily harm.

But the judge dismissed the case. He told the court, 'Surely any adult knows perfectly well that the dead cannot rise from their coffins. In any case, there is no rule that I am aware of which states that every coffin must contain a dead body.'

Weekend

Mr Leonard said PC Groves told the detectives, 'I was repairing her needlework-box and accidentally hit her on the head. Somehow it developed and I put my arms round her neck and strangled her. Have you ever had one of those days when nothing goes right?'

The Times

Twenty one-year-old Douglas Fairbairn poured a kettle of boiling water over his mother's head, a court was told yesterday, because he believed that his mother had neglected to call the television repair man.

Daily Mirror quoted in *New Statesman*'s 'This England'

SALE of excellent household furniture, piano, and marble bas relief of the 14th century, by Don A. Tello.

Chester Observer

When the express arrived the superintendent of the local Zoo was summoned, and after a three hours' struggle he was lassoed and pulled into a waiting cage.

Sunday Times

Among the side-reactions of this mercurial drug the most important is the death of the patient shortly after the injection.

New York State Medical Journal

The electrical equipment of the car is so arranged that the mere fact of wishing to inspect any of the high tension apparatus causes the whole of this to be connected to earth and thus made safe.

Railway News

Just to keep the record straight, it was the famous Whistler's Mother, not Hitler's, that was exhibited at the recent meeting of Pleasantville Methodists. There is nothing to be gained in trying to explain how the error occurred.

Titusville Herald (Pennsylvania)

The match was unfinished owing to measles. Craghurst was compelled to scratch.

The Harrovian

From Brig. Sir MARK HENNIKER

SIR – Mrs Mary Stewart-Wallace's letter (12 April), preferring 'referendums' and 'mediums' to 'referenda' and 'media', reminds me of the lightning reply made by a famous sapper, when a subaltern, to a pompous scientist.

The question was: 'Have you two officers completed your experiments with the pendula?'

The reply: 'Yes, sir. We are now sitting on our ba doing our sa.'

MARK HENNIKER

Letter to *Daily Telegraph*

```
I suffer so much from static electricity
in my clothes and on me that when I kiss
my boyfriend goodnight I give him violent
electric shocks which run up our noses!
There is a definite crackle and it really
hurts. My boyfriend is beginning to think
it's not worth it.
```

Letter in *Women's Mirror*

Note to schoolteacher: 'Please don't force Sheila to take her helping of cabbage at school meals. She just brings it home every day stuffed down her socks.'

Quoted in *Tit-Bits*

A woman who had a passport picture taken in a 'While-you-wait' photographer's in the West End was told to call back next day for the print.

She said she wanted to wait for it. The reply was: 'We only *take* the photograph while you wait.'

Evening Standard

It was a most beautiful catch by Hutchings in the deep field
on the leg side that dismissed Mr Sprot. The tree which
stands in the ground was too near to be pleasant, and Mr
Hutchings had to run back quickly and held it over his head.

The Times

20 MILES FROM BRIGHTON
LOVELY LITTLE GENTLEMAN'S
WEEK-END RESIDENCE

Advert in *Country Life*

Well-built modern house in 2 excellent self-contained flats.
An opportunity not to be missed. Bath vacant in the early
spring.

Advert in *Gloucester Echo*

Already disqualified from driving for life, 25-year-old
Joseph Morgan, unemployed, was disqualified for a further
seven years at Liverpool Crown Court.

Liverpool Echo

Today Patcham Tower windmill is minus one of its four
arms thanks to a high downland wind. The crash didn't
worry Mrs Joy Benson, aged 24, who is expecting a baby in
August. She had been half expecting it.

Brighton Argus

Another statement said: 'Some of the girls went to the bedrooms with the boys.' A third statement by a boy of 15 told how he went to the bedroom to get his coat and found a couple in bed together. It added: 'I could not find my coat so I went to the kitchen, got a breadknife and hit the piano.'

Yorkshire Post

Oldenburg, West Germany, 21 Jan. A 37-year-old woman has been found guilty of trying to kill her husband, even though he was already dead when she shot him.

Frau Ingrid Nicken was jailed for two years on a charge of attempted murder. She appealed against the verdict. According to evidence at the trial, she shot her husband twice in a rage after finding him sitting motionless in the kitchen one night after a drinking bout.

He had apparently died of a heart attack.

News agency

Life is certainly becoming more difficult. Even the hypochondriac can have little pleasure in his illness, for with the enormous increase in remedies there is the constant anxiety lest a cure be found for his particular complaint.

Letter in *British Medical Journal*

Mrs Swanney has very kindly presented an easel to hold the blackboard in the Church Hall. Not long ago she presented a cupboard to hold the china. We are very grateful to Mrs Swanney. A new piano is badly wanted in the hall . . .

Nelson Church Gazette

A safe and sound way to carry your favourite group and Mr Clarence Jackson (tenor), use an empty roll-on deodorant bottle, cleaned out well, and filled with cologne.

Trinidad Guardian

John Wilson had suffered from attacks of pneumonia and jaundice but, at Linton Hospital, near Maidstone, he died from arterial sclerosis. 'It will be a miracle if he ever paints again,' said his wife Barbara.

Sevenoaks Chronicle

He said one of the officers snatched the camera from a French boy who was taking photographs and exposed the film and tried to do the same thing to his wife.

Evening Post (Bristol)

Foraging parties of refugees have raided orchards and stripped cops up to five miles away.

Daily Telegraph

DOVER ROAD. Semi-det. house
with sea through lounge.

Folkestone, Hythe & District Herald

Under the baton of Mr S. Rutherford the Cosmopolitan Club orchestra provided musical numbers. Miss Maisie Robinson's outstanding features convulsed the audience.

Gisborne Herald

Sir, – Mr Green's interesting article: 'The trouble with
cockroaches', prompts the following story of an experience
of a friend of mine some years ago. Returning late from the
club one Saturday night he found everybody in bed, but his
kitchen floor alive with cockroaches. Being of a tidy mind he
sucked up as many as he could in a vacuum cleaner. Then
the thought that they were not dead but merely snug in the
cleaner prompted him to connect it by rubber tubing to a
gas tap, and to fill the cleaner with gas. He retired happily
to bed and slept late.

Next morning his wife found the cleaner and thought she
would clean up a little; she switched on and it promptly
blew up! The representative of the manufacturers was called
in, and he confessed that he had 'never seen one go like
that before'. My friend kept his silence and eventually got
his replacement vacuum cleaner. I dare say any surviving
cockroaches were highly amused. – R. J. MORLEY, 73
Egmont Rd, Sutton, Surrey.

Letter in New Scientist

Sir, – Mr W. S. Oglethorpe may be interested to know that
in France there are generally, to each basin or bath, two
taps marked respectively c and f. Experience tells me that
these letters stand for 'cold' and 'freezing' and on which
side the taps are so lettered appears to be quite immaterial.
– ALAN R. HILLS, 201 Broadway, Bexleyheath.

Letter in The Times

Madame Ivy Cannon, a charwoman employed at the
Ministry of War, has been given two years' imprisonment
plus a £500 fine for covering her jam-pots with top secret
military documents.

Paris-Presse

In the event of fire, the visitor, avoiding panic, is to walk
down the corridor and warm the chambermaid.

Notice in Dordogne hotel

WANTED, new pair of football boots, for a good young
fox-terrier dog.

Advert in *Our Dogs*

Dip your soiled face in alcohol, rinse it in the liquid and
hang it straight out to dry. It may then be pressed.

Toronto Mail

Late that same evening, after a vain search all round the
village, Mary found the dog dead in the garden. She
curried the body indoors.

Short story

Chairman of the Bench, Mr A. C. Bailey, told him: 'You
are now living in England, and we would like you to forget
this and live a decent and ordered life in future.'

Nelson Leader

Knocked down and badly injured by a motor-car in London
Road, Kingston, what is described as a sea-lion 8 ft long,
weighing about 6 cwt has been washed ashore near Fowey,
Cornwall.

Surrey paper

'BODY IN BOOT' CAR CHASE

A woman reported to Southend police today that she had
seen a car being driven at Leigh-on-Sea with what appeared
to be a body protruding from the open boot. Police found
the car – with two legs sticking out of the back. They
belonged to a garage mechanic trying to trace a noise
which was annoying the driver.

Evening Standard

PC'S FALSE TEETH MADE JP WONDER

The charge sheet read 'assaulting a police officer and wilfully damaging the constable's upper dentures'.

But the point that puzzled the magistrate at Greenwich
yesterday was how a man, who admitted cutting the policeman in the mouth, could have known he was wearing
dentures. And, said the magistrate, if the man did not know
about the constable's dentures, how could he wilfully
damage them?

Daily Mail

THE MUSICIAN MAKES HIMSELF GLIÈRE

You can Telemann by where he wants to live. I just Toch
a trip Orff into the Beethoven spaces Fauré Weick, and to
be Franck, it drove Menotti. Within a few days I was
Messiaen the city so Munch that, even though the weather
wasn't Clementi, I couldn't resist my Honegger to Galuppi
right Bach home early Satie. I know opinion Varèse; but
Vivaldi noise of the Bizet traffic, de Falla engines, and
knowing there are Mennin the streets Callas enough to
knock your Bloch off, I Haieff to say I still prefer the
Mitropoulos.

The Boyce were Sor I couldn't stand the Riegger out in
the Field, but I don't give a Schütz. I thought I'd lose my
continued on page 153

In accordance with his annual custom, an unknown benefactor walked into the cashier's office of the Church Army last week, handed over a cheque for £500 and left without waiting for thanks.

As great quantities of such parasites are about at this season, it may be useful to give a few hints as to how to exterminate them.

Western Daily Press

The man who would stoop so low as to write an anonymous letter, the least he could do would be to sign his name to it.

Letter in Irish paper

At a police-controlled crossing, drivers who wish to turn right should wait for the All Clear before running over the policeman.

Hamburger Nachrichten

ANTON

Saint-Saëns in the country. Let me Liszt the sounds: the
Rorem of the wind, the Lipatti, Patti, Tippett, Glinka,
Poulenc of the rain on the roof, the Massenet of the horses,
the Menuhin of the cats, the Gluck-Gluck of the wood-
peckers Chopin holes in the Bartök, the incessant Tcherpnin
of a Byrd in a nearby Grofé, and every morning Lecocq
crows.

I got poison Ives when a Wolf chased me into a brio
Partch. I'm no Robeson Caruso. I could have died of
Borodin talking to the Babbitt. A friend said the country
was the best place to live; Abegg his pardon. Another
friend said he didn't like it in those Gotterdämmerung
Hills; I agree, only Morceau. Not for all the Gould and
Diamond would I go back.

I don't Cherubini for the Ruggles life. I like a full Méhul
three times a day, a dry Martinu and Szigeti at Joe's. I like
to Locatelli in the evenings. Is that asking for Egk in
Meyerbeer? Nono! In fact, I Ravel in the Bliss of urban
existence. So many Weber under a Holst of problems they
feel they can't Handel. Their answer is too Offenbach to
nature – into Haydn I call it. I carry on a d'Indy life in this
Berg. Délibes me.

James W. Pruett, University of North Carolina
From *Notes*, the Journal of the American
Music Library Association

NOTICE

£5 REWARD. – Whereas some person or persons
stabbed my Donkey on the 26th of January, and well-
known about Town, and has since died through the wound
inflicted. I hereby offer the above Reward to any person
giving any information concerning the cruel deed.

WILLIAM CAMERON, Cape Town, 1881
Journalistic Jumbles

Can you advise me what can be done to rid my house of
earwigs? Last year we were alive with them. We used to
find them on our bed, and used to run down the wall and
across the table at mealtimes.

                                        Letter in *Amateur Gardening*

Sir Henry — was presented today with the honorary
Freedom of Plymouth. The magistrate remanded him in
custody 'in order to get the alcohol out of his system'.

                                        Evening paper

Mr Johnson was pinned to the ground receiving injuries to
his right leg, body and shoulder. What was most trying of
all, his lighted cigarette rested on the side of his cheek, near
his eye, and he could not move it.

   Look out for the repeat performance.

                                        Yorkshire Post

In the past, the Council had felt that the first thing they
should do was to get the storm water out of the sewers before
trying to force home-owners in. It was decided at last night's
meeting that where the sewers could take the waste water
without flooding, the owners should be told to get in now.

                                        Bryan Times (Ohio)

Practise thinning in winter time and head back in summer.
A tree can be kept bearing practically regular crops. Of
course it is impossible to keep any tree bearing practically
regular crops, but of course it is impossible to keep any tree
bearing a full crop regularly. Wonders can be done by this
system of pruning.

                                        Nurseryman's leaflet

But even the Eindhoven experience can't hold a candle to what happened when a hi-fi firm demonstrated its new radio receiver to a crowded room at a British hi-fi show. The radio had been pre-tuned to a respectable BBC station so that when the demonstrator pressed the requisite switch the room would fill and thrill to the sound of hi-fi radio reproduction. Dead on cue the radio receiver sprang obediently into life but caught just the last three words of a sentence. '. . . tits like coconuts' boomed the hi-fi system. A subsequent check with the *Radio Times* explained all. The verbal snatch had come from a discussion between experts on the feeding habits of wild birds.

New Scientist

Middleborough, Mass, lies 34 miles S by E from Boston, 14 miles SSW from Plymouth, and 10 SE from Taunton. Incorporated 1660. Population, 5005.

In 1763, Shubael Thompson found a land turtle, marked on the shell J.W., 1747. Thompson marked it and let it go. Elijah Clapp found it in 1773; William Shaw found it in 1775; Jonathan Soule found it in 1790, and Zenas Smith, in 1791: each marked it with his initials. Whether the *critter* is dead or gone to the west, we have no account.

Robb's Cabinet of Curiosities

A grindstone ordered from England in 1898 was delivered to the customer in Bunbury, Western Australia, in August 1962. The ship in which it was being transported had sunk sixty-four years earlier, and the grindstone had been salvaged by an underwater explorers 'club.

Reveille

Lassalle fell in love in a few moments, carried the woman of his choice down exactly three flights of stairs, and then, as though his intellect had interfered to dampen his emotions, he let the whole matter drop.

From *Genius and Character* by Emil Ludwig

By an unfortunate typographical error we were made to say last week that the retiring Mr D— was a member of the defective branch of the police force. Of course this should have read: 'The detective branch of the police farce.'

New Zealand paper

The Night of the Generals
OMAR SHARIF, PETER O'TOOLE
The story of a strange manhunt for a psychopathic kipper set against the background of wartime Paris.

TV Scene

Mr and Mrs Joseph T. Fraser Jr, of Philadelphia, are pictured here in Delphi, Greece, where they exploded antiquities.

Caption in *Philadelphia Inquirer*

To emphasize the shape of the eyes, pencil in a fine brown line actually following the growth of the lashes. Mascara must be made into a nice creamy consistency and lower lashes made up well with lemon curd and ice the top with lemon water icing, or sprinkle icing sugar on top.

Greenock Telegraph

Sir, – In last Sunday's issue you published a reproduction
of Dame Laura Knight's boxing sketch of one of the
successful entries in the Olympic Games Fine Arts Competition, to be seen in the Sport in Art Exhibition at the
Victoria and Albert Museum.

My Association controls and regulates amateur boxing at
the Olympic Games and in the 41 countries who are
affiliated to us; and I therefore feel it my duty to point out
that the boxers in the sketch are committing the following
offences: (1) Holding; (2) Improper use of the hand (both
boxers); (3) Extending a stiff arm under the opponent's
arm; (4) 'Wrestling'. It is possible that the boxers are also
delivering the kidney punch and the rabbit punch, but one
cannot be certain of this.

I do not presume to criticize the sketch as a work of art,
but it is regrettable that an exhibition which is designed to
portray amateur sport in its highest forms should have
included an example which degrades the noble art of self-
defence to the level of a free-for-all rough and tumble.
Yours, etc., RUDYARD H. RUSSELL, Lt-Col., Honorary
Secretary-Treasurer, Association Internationale de Boxe
Amateur.

Letter in the *Observer*

The Chairman told Middlesex executive committee of the
Health Service, yesterday, that a set of false teeth was found
stuck in a meringue behind a tree at Buckingham Palace
after a garden party.

Daily Express

BREAKS BOTH LEGS TURNING OVER IN BED

Headline in *The World*

Hampshire elected to bath first on a pitch damp on top
from the early morning rain.

Wolverhampton Express and Star

A 38-year-old woman was mugged and robbed of her
shopping bag in Joseph Street, Derby, yesterday. She was
taken to Derbyshire Royal Infirmary, but later allowed
home, after being rabbit-punched in the back of the neck.

Derby Evening Telegraph

The creature resembles a minnow, has a thin skin with
netlike markings, a primitive digestive system and a
rudimentary stiffening rod which appears to be the pre-
decessor of a backbone.

He has been in the US Army since Thanksgiving Day
1968.

Dallas Times Herald

10.00 Women Are Revolting.
One-hour special.

Boston Herald Traveler

Dr Garside said that after the accident Williams did several
of the tests quite well. Williams told him he had been to a
very good dinner and had a good deal to drink at it. He was
certain that his car had touched nothing.

Bristol Evening Post

Mrs Lukes was caught beneath the auto and taken to St
Joseph's Hospital with several fractured bones. The bones
were on their way to Woonsocket to spend their holiday.

Connecticut paper

DENTIST GOES UP THE POLE

CLEVELAND, Monday – A dentist is to climb up to
Charley Lupica of Cleveland, the pole-sitter who has been
squatting for ninety days to prove his faith in the Cleveland
Indians baseball team. Lupica has toothache and will have
a temporary filling to last him until he comes down.

News Agency

Will the person who unknown to me returned the family
album, horseshoe ring, 72-inch pearl beads, 2 side combs set
with brilliants, 36-inch pearl beads, PLEASE RETURN the
25th photograph of the condemned building corner Ivins
and Oak Avenues, opposite city line. Reward. Apply —.

Advert in Philadelphia Record

WOMAN OF 71 BANNED FROM WALKING RACE

A grandmother aged 71 was banned yesterday from a
Yorkshire mining village's Bank Holiday walk because
officials said she was a professional athlete.

Eastmid News Service

Sir, – I would like to offer another remedy for 'clogged
feet' in dreams – with me it always succeeds.

Whenever I am overcome in this way I immediately un-
screw my feet at the ankles, and hurry on without them.
One must, however, remember that the left foot has a
left-hand thread.

Yours faithfully,
H. R. F. KEATING, Dublin
Daily Telegraph

Mr Barden spoke with an eloquence which sprang from his deep-seated conviction of the grave pass which we have reached, basing his proposals upon the significant memorandum which the Almighty had prepared at his request.

Montreal Gazette

There is one such building now being erected within a few miles of Manchester as the cock crows.

Manchester paper

It would be a great help towards keeping the churchyard in good order if others would follow the example of those who clip the grass on their own graves.

Parish magazine

Save time and cut fingers with a parsley mincer.

This Week

Coo forty-five minutes and cover with a layer of sliced tomatoes. Season lightly with salt and pepper and coo until meat is very tender.

Beverly Hills Shopping News

The operation is relatively safe, the scientists said. It has been tried on about 30 dogs. Five of them are alive and well.

Washington Post

Formerly a don at Oxford, he developed later an interest in education, and migrated to Ontario.

Canadian Review

Mrs Kitty Clark Birks – I would like to communicate
with you, object going 315 miles north with you – George.

The World

A father is seeking insurance cover against his 16-year-old
daughter losing her virginity before she marries. But he is
unlikely to succeed, for in a historic ruling last night,
Lloyd's of London ruled: 'Loss of virginity is a moral
hazard, and so uninsurable.'

The anxious father, it would appear, is not so much
worried about his daughter's purity, but about the financial
burden he will have to bear if she does lose her most price-
less possession. For he comes from Sicily, where there are
strong views about chastity, and a non-virgin is unlikely to
get married. He is now living in Bolzano, Northern Italy,
but his daughter wants to go and work as a waitress in
Germany. Father has agreed – on condition that she first
gets 'fully comprehensive insurance'.

He went to the nearest city, Innsbruck, in Austria, and
asked the largest insurance company there to carry out a
medical check on his daughter and then issue a policy –
premiums 27s a month – giving him £575 if the worst
comes to the worst. Perplexed, the company sent the file to
Lloyd's, where a spokesman said: 'This is the strangest
request ever.'

Sun

When examined by the Divisional Surgeon, defendant was
very abusive and when asked to clench his teeth, he took
them out, gave them to the doctor and said, 'You clench
them.'

Woking Herald & News

Discovered at 5.06 a.m., the flames starting on the third floor of the Midwest Salvage Co. spread so rapidly that the first firemen on the scene were driven back to safety and leaped across three streets to ignite other buildings.

Cincinnati Times Star

Dr Reuben contended, 'The tragedy is that sex education in medical schools is far from adequate and most of today's doctors can't provide satisfactory answers to the questions put to them by their parents.'

American Medical News

Friends of mine asked a hotel for a quiet room overlooking
the river. The hotel provided one with a tranquil view over
the gentle stream, the water meadows and the bridge. They
did not mention, however, that the bridge was going to be
blown up by demolition men at a quarter to seven the next
morning.

Punch

The other morning you reported that a small quantity
of washing powder put in a duckpond would make all the
ducks sink to the bottom.

My neighbour's little boy put a whole packet in, but the
ducks still went on swimming. It makes you wonder if you
can believe everything you read in the newspapers.

Letter in *Birmingham Gazette*

Sir, – An article in today's issue discusses how to send a
message from an express train. Faced with the same
problem on the same line, I consulted the steward in charge
of the dining car. He provided me with pencil and paper,
made an incision in a large potato, and himself lobbed the
potato to the feet of a porter as we ran through Peterborough, with my message wedged in it but clearly visible.
The stationmaster did what was necessary.

The steward would not take anything: he was glad to be
of service.

Yours faithfully, H. C. B. MYNORS,
Sutton Green, Guildford.

The Times

*This Appliance
will reduce your
Hips, or Bust*

Advert in *People's Home Journal*

OLD ENGLISH SHEEPDOG – male, 6 mo, AKC Ch sired, white faced, pick of litter, all leather interior. Mechanically excellent.

Advert in *New York Times*

A lion was badly mauled in Intra, Italy, yesterday by a woman who escaped from her kitchen.

Irish News

Mrs Oscar Maddox is able to be up after being confined to bed for several weeks with malaria fever, to the delight of her friends.

Thomasville Times-Enterprise (Georgia)

The Nebraska legislature was asked to enact a law providing annulment of marriages of all couples who do not within three years after the wedding have one or more children by Representative Hines, Democrat of Omaha, who is a bachelor.

Radio news aboard *USS Pennsylvania*

A 67-year-old retired labourer, John Whiting, went to Durham Magistrates' Court yesterday to testify he was alive. 'Are you dead?' he was asked. 'I am not,' Mr Whiting replied.

Daily Mail

On the same bus as myself was a schoolboy whose head had become stuck in a vase. His mother was rushing him off to hospital. Presumably to avoid attracting attention she had placed her son's school cap on top of the vase.

Letter in *John Bull*, quoted in *New Statesman*

The letter, which was read by the magistrate, Mr John Hooper, stated that a near relative of Dr S— had cut off his hands, stabbed him to death, cut up his body and taken the pieces back to Iraq to show his family. The letter ended: 'We are all very sorry and are sure that he did not intend to do anything wrong, but it was just bad luck.'

Coulsdon and Purley Advertiser

A man whose car crashed into a telegraph pole agreed at Epsom County Court today that he should pay the expense incurred by the Post Office for installing a new post, but claimed that he was entitled to the old one. 'As I am paying for the new post I should at least be allowed to take the old one away,' said Mr William Joseph Mitten, of St Clair Drive, Worcester Park.

Judge Gordon Clark said: 'You cannot acquire telegraph poles simply by knocking them down.'

Evening Standard

LOST, Fri. night, between Oughtibridge and Hillsboro', a small red-faced Lady's wristwatch; sentimental value.

Sheffield Star

Among the first to enter was Mrs Clara Adams of Erie, Pa., lone woman passenger. Slowly her nose was turned around to face in a south-westerly direction away from the hangar doors. Then like some strange beast, she crawled along the grass.

California paper

Mr and Mrs Benny Croset announce the birth of a little son which arrived on the 5.15 last Thursday.

West Union People's Defender (Oregon)

The projector was worked by Mr Moore and Mr Gordon and when the light failed through the bulb fusing Mr Boyd explained that seals do not drink salt water.

Kilmarnock Standard

A Lewes, Sussex Corporation clerk has been sentenced to 18 months' imprisonment for stealing 14,000 new penny pieces from Eastbourne public lavatories. He spent the pennies on high living.

Irish Times

My weekly treat is a visit to a small local cinema. The manager there knows almost every customer. I have a seat booked at the end of the back row and, as I suffer from bad feet, the manager allows me the luxury of bathing my feet in hot water during the show. I fill up the bowl in his office. You do not get service like this in the big posh cinemas.

Letter in *Reveille*

Apparatus for removing casings from sausages and the like
(U.S. Patent No. 2,672,646)
In a sausage-skinning machine, means for rotating a sausage about its longitudinal axis, means for simultaneously holding a part of the skin against rotative movement with the sausage to cause said skin to be torn off said sausage circumferentially, and means for simultaneously moving said sausage endwise with respect to said holding means, said rotating, holding and moving means being operatively related to one another to cause said skin to be torn off and stripped from the sausage helically.

In order to maintain a high standard of service to our customers, this branch will be closed all day on Thursdays.

Sign in Walton-on-Thames shop

Zoologists could only visit the hot springs in El Hamma with the permission of the local Kaliphat and with an escort of police, since it is reserved for the exclusive use of Muslim women bathers. An attempt was made to bring back a number of specimens alive in vacuum flasks so that further investigation could be carried out in Oxford.

Illustrated London News

To repair damaged tablecloths, first lay the tablecloth flat, with the hole uppermost.

Dublin Evening Mail

Man critical after
bus backs into him
Middleton Press (Connecticut)

Add the remainder of the milk, beat again, turn quickly into buttered pans and bake half an hour. Have the oven hot, twist a length of narrow green ribbon around them and you have a pretty bouquet for your dress or hat.

Barrow News

Mrs Alice McCrory and son, Harvey, went to Dayton last Sunday to visit Mr and Mrs Carl Dunbar, who were slightly injured in an automobile accident last week. Mrs Dunbar before her accident was Miss Olivia McCrory.

Ohio paper

My husband is a shy man and whenever he brings flowers home to me he always conceals them under his bowler hat.

As a result they have to be little flowers like violets or anemones and tend to smell of brilliantine.

Surely there must be some other way in which self-conscious men cope with this problem?

Letter in Today

Mrs L. Smith of Alma Street, Aston, Birmingham, said in evidence that while picnicking she saw the horse chase a couple up the river bank and then eat their sandwiches. She threw her coat over her own and her husband's sandwiches, but the horse ate through it to get at the food. Her husband complained to the Town Council.

The Times

For forty years Jim Martin earned a living in vaudeville letting people swing a 10-lb sledge-hammer at a 50-lb rock balanced on his head. He thinks that one day there might be a new demand for this form of entertainment. So, just in case, he keeps in training by beating his bald head with blocks of wood every morning.

Reynolds News

Dear Editor, – Thank you for the lovely, sane letter about telling the little ones. With a box of seeds planted in the window, a mother cat with two babies under my kitchen stove, and your wonderful letter tucked away in my desk I feel ready for anything.

Pictorial Review

Dig the ground over thoroughly and then pant.

Gardening article

He could see a dim red tail-light about a mile ahead of him. Oliver switched off his own lights and rammed down the accelerator with clenched teeth.

From a short story

A son was born during the past week to Mr and Mrs William Kleintop, Leigh Avenue. Congratulations, Pete!

Palmerton Press (Pennsylvania)

Sow seeds now in moderately fertile soil which has been lightly limed. If birds or mice are troublesome in your garden guard against them by shaking them in a paper bag with some red lead.

Marlborough Express (N.Z.)

Sir, I had such a nice, such an unexpected present yesterday that I feel I must tell you about it. On to the small pool (20 ft) in this London garden there suddenly swooped down a duck and a drake. They swam around for perhaps ten minutes and then had a little siesta. When they departed I found, left presumably as a courteous 'thank-you', an egg. It made a delicious breakfast.
Yours truly, ALEC CLIFTON-TAYLOR

Sir, I don't want to spoil Alec Clifton-Taylor's memory of a delicious breakfast (April 17), but if the duck which laid his egg was of a wild species, eating its egg was an offence under section 1(c) of the Protection of Birds Act 1954.
Yours faithfully, DAVID GREEN

Sir, Mr David Green (April 21) may have overlooked the fact that the egg was unsolicited by Mr Clifton-Taylor (letter, April 17). Therefore under section 1 of the Unsolicited Goods and Services Act, 1971, if the egg is not repossessed by the sender within six months, the recipient may deal with it as if it were an unconditional gift.

Some may consider Mr Clifton-Taylor to have acted prematurely. However, if not dealt with promptly, the egg would have become a nuisance and Mr Clifton-Taylor is entitled to prevent this.
Yours faithfully, ALAN BREWER

Sir, Mr Clifton-Taylor (April 17) acted hastily. If he had taken the egg indoors and kept it warm he might have ended up with lunch for four instead of breakfast for one.
Yours, etc. RONALD DAVIS

Letters in *The Times*

Q. *How can you tell the age of a snake?*
A. It is extremely difficult to tell the age of a snake unless
   you know exactly when it was born.

Detroit News

VENICE – Argentine water-painter Nicola Garcia Uriburu,
armed with an authorization from antipollution authorities,
dumped colour into the Grand Canal and turned bright
green briefly.

Long Island Press

FOR RENT
Three bedroomed house, furnished,
refrigerator near the bus stop

Barbados Advocate

They delivered 66 food parcels to the elderly residents living
locally in a large box.

Harlow Gazette and Citizen

A mirror worth £5 was stolen from a showhouse on a
building site in Congleton on Saturday afternoon. Police
are looking into it.

Congleton Chronicle

If you are satisfactory,
tell your friends. If you
are unsatisfactory, warn
the waitress.

Notice in Bulgarian hotel

When Mrs Janet Trent opened her diary yesterday the entry for the day was already filled in by someone else and read: 'House burgled 5 a.m.' A burglar had stolen £24 as she slept in her Hallfield Estate, Paddington, home.

Daily Express

Corned beef was sent to a Bridgend school canteen. Teachers sniffed it and did not like it. A canteen manageress sniffed it, but pronounced it good; the town sanitary inspector sniffed it and passed it as good; the town medical officer sniffed it and declared it good – then ordered it to be destroyed because too many people had sniffed it.

Daily Express

Sir, Today I took the necessary documents for the renewal of my car licence to the local post office. A very polite young man examined the documents and said: 'Sir, I am sorry I cannot give you a new licence as you have not given me the reminder letter from the Vehicle Licensing Department.'

'I have had no reminder letter,' I replied. 'This year I have remembered.'

'I am sorry, Sir, but you must produce a reminder letter,' he answered. 'I suggest that the only thing for you to do is to write to the Vehicle Licensing Department reminding them to send you a reminder letter.' *Quis custodiet?*

Yours sincerely, JOHN COWLEY

Letter in *The Times*

The family's youngest daughter, Lady Diana, recalls that the house is 'beautiful but very simple'. This, too, is the impression that many people gain of Lady Home herself.

Yorkshire Post

Salisbury magistrates gave a Bulford man a conditional discharge when he appeared on a theft charge because they were impressed by the way he was trying to help himself.

Southern Evening Echo

We sent sixty dresses to Miss Forsythe in December, and we have just heard that she is using our gift in roofing the Mission House.

Report of Hibernian Church Missionary Society

She wore a black dress with a white front and she wrinkled up her face in a mischievous smile as her daughter pinned a rose on it so she would look nice for the picture.

Canadian paper

The native inhabitants produce all manner of curios, the great majority of which appear to command a ready sale among the visitors, crude and commonplace as these frequently are.

Bulawayo Chronicle

Can someone tell me if there is anyone who accepts newspapers? I save mine for the Council bin men but did not realize that they just throw men in the cart to be ground up with all other rubbish. This seems shocking.

Letter in *Hartlepool Mail*

AMOROUS BULL'S ADVENTURES CUT SHORT

A farmer who castrated his neighbour's amorous bull has been fined in Johannesburg for malicious damage. Jan Hendrix Lubbe said that the bull, which was diseased, kept jumping over his fence and copulating with his cows, infecting five of them.

The last time the bull came visiting, Lubbe became so angry that he cornered it and castrated it.

The magistrate, Mr W. J. P. Marais, said he sympathized with Lubbe, but he should not take the law into his own hands. 'The bull was only answering the call of nature.' Lubbe, who pleaded not guilty, was fined £50 or 80 days' jail, suspended for three years.

Agency tape

PRESSMEN GATHER TO SEE
ROYALS HUNG AT WINDSOR

Sunday Times

Dr Addison, who is a leading authority on this important subject, will speak on the general questions of weed control and Miss Thompson will follow with a short talk on the control of wild oats of which she has made a special study.

A committee notice

Another bomb was found at Sydney's central railway station. Police, who put an extra guard on Prince Philip, said, 'We are dealing with a madman.'

Financial Times quoted in
Another batch of boobs from Private Eye

In Elmfield Avenue, Teddington, last Saturday cigarette ash falling in the cat's box caused a small fire. Little damage was done and the blaze was put out by the occupier.

Surrey Comet

A tight hat can be stretched. First damp the head with steam from a boiling kettle.

Scots paper

'I knew then that what I dreaded – that I would talk under torture – was a thing of the past. I knew that I was a MAN.'

The writer of that letter gets our first prize of six pairs of nylons.

Week-end Mail